1

The sun was so hot. Joy and I tried to shade our faces as we walked.

"I really feel sorry for Priscilla," Joy said as she licked her ice cream cone. "Just because she's pregnant, and had dropped out of school — now there is not one person who wants to be her friend."

"So, why don't *you* be her friend?" I asked.

"*Me?* Listen, I feel sorry for her, but I can't be her friend. What would we talk about? Her mind is on her baby, and my mind is on school and fun." Then Joy looked thoughtful as she added, "I wonder; will her baby stay with her, or with the guy who made her pregnant."

"Probably the guy's parents will take it," I said.

"It must be terrible," Joy continued, "I mean, to give birth to a baby and then see it taken away to another home."

"But what else can she do?"

"I really don't know," Joy said sadly. Then she

quickly added, "While I'm still in school, you'll never find me pregnant!"

"Nor me," I agreed.

Suddenly Joy looked at her watch and exclaimed, "I must run! Mother told me to be home in time to cook."

"But don't you have time to go to Dan's with me?"

"Sorry, Sindie, not today," she said as she quickly turned and rushed off.

I waved good-bye and continued walking to Dan's. I had to go there. My mother told me to bring home two bottles of Coke.

The real name is "Dan's Quick Foods." It's a favourite place for us teenagers. Joy and I go there almost every day. Dan's has a dozen tables where you can sit and eat a hamburger or just have a cold drink. Sometimes we spend an hour slowly sipping Cokes and talking about everything and everyone.

Joy is my very best friend. We always understand each other. And we have no secrets. I tell her everything, and she never looks down on me. We spend all our free time together.

The only difference between Joy and me is: She's beautiful. She has a pretty face and perfectly shaped legs. Mine are much too thin.

People say I'm pretty, but it's hard for me to believe. By age 16 a girl's body should have a nice shape, but me . . . I'm all bones! Maybe I'm not ugly, but I'm certainly not like Joy. Whenever boys turn to look at us, I know they are looking only at her.

When I reached Dan's, I bought the Coke and then I heard a low voice saying, "Hello, Sweet Baby. Let me carry those heavy bottles for you."

HELLO SWEET BABY

A story of passion and intrigue.

*Romantically he whispered,
"I'll phone you some time."*

Bruce and Carol
BRITTEN

OASIS INTERNATIONAL LTD
Wheaton, Illinois
USA
Jos, Plateau State
Nigeria

INSIGHT BOOKS
AFRICAN ISSUES AFRICA'S AUTHORS

Hello Sweet Baby

ISBN: 978-1-59452-006-8
ISBN: 1-59452-006-2

Cover design by Robyn Martins

Oasis International is a ministry devoted to fostering a robust and sustainable pan-African publishing industry. For more information, go to oasisint.net.

Looking up I saw a sharply-dressed guy with broad shoulders and a wonderful smile. "No, thanks. I can carry them myself," I told him.

Gently he took one of the bottles while saying, "Okay, you carry one and I'll carry the other."

I don't know why I didn't hold the bottles tightly and tell him to go away. I'm always careful to show no interest when guys try to sweet-talk me. But this guy was different. Somehow he was special. Perhaps it was his good looks and his confident voice.

My home is not far from Dan's — so we walked together for only five minutes. "I arrived in this little town yesterday," he told me. "My home is in the city of Malesus. For the school holiday I'm staying here with my aunt."

My heart dropped as I realised: He will leave in just two months, and then I may never see him again!

Before we reached my home, he handed me the other bottle and said, "I hope I'll see you tomorrow at the same time."

I continued walking, and without looking back at him I just said, "Maybe."

Smiling to myself, I realised: I don't even know his name. Yet in my mind I could still see his handsome body full of muscles. I felt like I was in a wonderful dream.

When I reached home, I threw open the kitchen door and said very cheerfully, "How are you, Mom? Let me help you do that."

She stopped peeling potatoes and looked up at me in surprise. Usually she had to *tell* me to help with dinner. "Thanks, Sindie. Please cut up that cabbage. I hope you remember that Ruth and her husband are going to church this evening, and you promised to take care of their little boy."

"Oh that's right!" I had completely forgotten. "I really must *hurry!"*

Suddenly my mind had no more time to think about *him.* Mom and I rushed to cook. After dinner I hurried to Ruth's house. I always enjoy taking care of her little son, Joel. He is age two and so *sweet!*

Ruth and her husband are the two nicest people on earth! They make me feel so relaxed. I can be myself when I'm with them.

The only thing I don't like about them is: Often they talk about God.

Yet, I really like the way love shines in their eyes as they laugh and joke with each other. That's the kind of marriage I want someday.

Ruth is the only adult I can speak to freely, but I decided not to tell her that I met a guy at Dan's.

The following morning I woke up with a glorious feeling — knowing I was going to see *him* again.

Then fear suddenly hit me as I told myself, "Perhaps he won't show up. Maybe he talked to me just to be polite. Maybe he really thinks I'm ugly!"

I sat on the edge of my bed. What should I do? Should I get ready to meet him, or not?

After washing and dressing, I decided: I must go to Dan's in the afternoon, just in case. How I hoped he would keep his promise to meet me there!

I left home right after lunch, hoping I looked nice. Along the way I kept checking myself in the mirrors created by the shop windows.

As I walked down the final hill, my shoes made a loud *slap . . . slap* sound that really embarrassed me.

Then I heard a wonderful voice saying, "I hope all that noise is coming to me."

Looking up I saw a very handsome guy leaning against the wall.

"Do you like noise?" I asked with a smile.

"I do if the noise is as pretty as you." He was smiling too.

"I'm not noise. I'm Sindie," I said, standing in front of him.

"Good afternoon, Sindie," he said, holding out his right hand.

I didn't shake his hand. Instead I turned my head and said in a playful voice, "I can't shake hands with someone I don't know."

"Oh, I'm sorry," his smile grew even wider. "My name's Ben. Now that the introductions are over, what do you say to a Coke?"

"If I say something to a Coke, do you think it will understand?" I joked.

Laughing, he said, "Okay, Sweet Baby. Would you like to *drink* a Coke with me?"

"Sure," I smiled. "Let's go."

We chose a table near the back, and as we slowly sipped our cold drinks, we talked about all the usual things. His father works for the railway; mine is an electrician. He has three sisters. I have an elder brother and a younger sister.

Actually, we didn't spend much time talking. Mostly we joked and laughed. I did learn that he enjoys jazz music, and he discovered that I love ice cream.

Although we didn't talk much, by the end of the

afternoon I felt like I really knew him. As we parted, he whispered, "I'll phone you some time."

"Bye," I said as I turned to walk home. My heart was so excited, I felt like my feet were floating above the earth!

Yet I wondered: Will he really phone me?

"I hope so," I said softly to myself. *"Oh, I hope so!"*

2

The next morning I told myself, "Ben will never phone me. A guy always tells a girl, *'I'll phone you,'* even if he never plans to speak to her again."

I felt so down-hearted. I wanted to phone Joy, but I couldn't think of what to say to her. I could only think of Ben. What did I do to make him never want to see me again?

Suddenly the phone rang. "Hello," I said . . . hoping, my heart beating wildly.

"What's happening?" his deep voice said playfully.

My voice shook a little. "What do you mean?"

"I've just come from Dan's, and the person I wanted to see wasn't there."

Relief filled my heart. "Who were you looking for?" I joked.

"You, of course."

I couldn't speak. I could only think: *He's been waiting for me!*

"So, what do you say? Are you coming to meet me, or not?"

"Yes. I can be there in an hour," I said excitedly. I was only half dressed, and my hair was a terrible mess.

Ben became silent. I feared he may have decided not to wait for me. "An hour," he said, disappointed. "All right, I'll wait here."

"Okay, good-bye."

Hanging up the phone, I ran to my wardrobe, chose a pretty dress, and did my hair faster than ever. My heart *over-flowed.* He actually phoned me!

As I left the house, I tried to walk normally, hoping my excitement wouldn't show. When I arrived at Dan's, Ben was standing near the door. "What took so long?" he asked impatiently.

I looked at my watch. "Only fifty minutes. What's your hurry?"

"I wanted to see you before I go back home today."

My heart dropped. He was leaving!

"I'll be away only four days," he continued. "I'm returning Friday noon. Can I meet you Friday evening?"

"I'm sorry," I said sadly. "I promised to take care of Ruth's little boy that evening. She and her husband are going to a birthday party."

"Who's Ruth?" Ben demanded.

"She's a friend."

Suddenly I had an idea. "Listen, why don't you come there? Ruth and her husband will leave early. Then I'll put Joel to bed at sundown. So if you come after that…"

"I'll be there," Ben broke in eagerly.

On a scrap of paper I drew a map showing how to get to Ruth's house. He looked at it, nodded, and shoved it in his shirt pocket. Then he smiled at me and said, "See you Friday."

My heart felt so excited, I didn't see him walk away, and I didn't see Joy coming towards me.

"Who's that handsome guy?" she asked with a big smile.

"That's Ben," I answered, trying to act as if I had no interest in him.

Joy invited me to go shopping with her, and the whole time she kept asking questions about Ben. I continued pretending to have no interest in him, but I'm sure she could see my true feelings.

Thursday passed so slowly. Sometimes I thought I couldn't wait another minute to see him.

When Friday finally arrived, I decided not to tell Ruth about Ben. Usually I tell her everything, but in this case I knew she would say, *"No, it's not right for you to be in a house alone with a boy."* But Ben and I wouldn't do anything wrong. And I wanted so badly to see him.

After I put Joel to bed, I looked at the clock every minute. I picked up one magazine after another, turning pages without seeing them.

Then, finally, there was a knock.

I hurried to unlock the door.

Ben looked confident as usual. "Did you have a nice trip?" I asked.

"Of course not," he said with a smile.

"Why not?"

"Because I missed you," he whispered romantically.

Then he put his arm around my waist as we sat down together.

"I missed you too," I said softly. I was too shy to look at his face. I just stared at the floor. Gently he took my chin in his hand and turned it up to his face. "Did you really?" he whispered.

I nodded my head and smiled.

His kiss was soft and gentle. I thought I would melt with excitement!

Then he looked at me and said, "I knew it."

"You knew what?" I asked, afraid he didn't like my kiss.

He kissed me again and said, "The first time I saw you, I knew your kiss would be sweet."

I just smiled, and he kissed me again.

Then he handed me a small parcel and said, "While I was home, I heard a new song. It tells exactly how I feel about you. So I bought the CD for you."

"Thanks!" I exclaimed. I removed the plastic as I headed for Ruth's CD player. "Which song is it?"

"The first one. It's called, *I'll Never Leave You.*"

I switched it on. Then I sat down near Ben again. He put his arm around me and pulled me even closer as we listened to the sweet music.

You are my dream, my life, my love.
I'll never leave you.
I love you today and forever.
I'll never leave you.
I'll always be near.
I'll never leave you, my love.

"That's beautiful!" I whispered,

For the rest of the evening we sat and talked. He continued kissing me, and his hand rested lightly on my thigh. It was so exciting — yet I was glad he didn't try to do anything more than just kiss.

Ben made me feel so loved. I wanted the evening to go on forever. I felt like I was floating high above the earth. It was the most sensational feeling I've ever had. Never before in my whole life had I felt such *love*.

I guess my parents love me, but they don't show it much. Anyway, parents must love a child. But Ben was a handsome guy, and he thought I was special.

When the time came for him to leave, I let go of his hand reluctantly. We promised to meet the following day at Dan's.

After he was gone, worry rushed into my mind and

chased away all my wonderful feelings. Why did I allow him to touch my thigh? And since when am I the kind of girl who fears that my parents may discover what I'm doing?

The next morning I succeeded in brushing off all those worries. My mind returned to thinking only of Ben.

Days began flying quickly past, and nearly every day Ben and I spent time together. We shopped . . . we played tennis . . . we walked . . . we ate ice cream. Sometimes we had serious talks, but mostly we joked and laughed.

At home I listened again and again to *our* song.

One day when Ben and I were walking in town, I saw Joy and I realised my friendship with her was cooling. But I didn't care. I cared only for Ben.

Then came the day that changed my whole life. It came after I had known Ben for two weeks, although it seemed we had known each other much longer.

I was sitting at home thinking that ice cream would taste good on such a hot day . . . then the phone rang.

"Hello."

"Hi, Sweet Baby. How about ice cream?"

"I'd love it!"

"Can you meet me in ten minutes?"

"Not ten . . . nine!"

"Okay, Baby."

As I fixed my hair I thought, "Something in his voice sounded different . . . smoother than usual. But maybe I'm just imagining it."

"Mom, may I go for ice cream?" I shouted from my room.

"Okay, Sindie," and then she added playfully, "You will grow *fat* from so much ice cream."

Mom always *assumed* I was meeting *Joy.* She didn't know about Ben.

When I arrived at Dan's, I saw Ben holding a half-eaten cone in one hand, and in the other a melting chocolate one . . . my favourite flavour!

And he was licking my chocolate cone!

"Wait!" I complained. "Your tongue is attracted to my cone."

"How do you know it's yours, Sweet Baby?"

Laughing, I took the cone from him before he could eat any more of it.

The day was awfully hot, but as we walked the cold, delicious ice cream cooled our veins.

"You love ice cream, don't you, Sindie?"

"I sure do," I agreed.

"Just think how your life would be if your parents told you, 'Never taste ice cream until you reach age 25.' Imagine if you waited and waited — then at 25 you tried it and found, 'I love it!' Wouldn't you say, 'Why didn't I try it sooner?'"

"What do you mean, Ben?"

"Today, my Sweet Baby, I want you to try a new experience. It's as good as ice cream. Better, in fact."

"I don't know what you're talking about," I said, hoping he didn't mean what I thought he meant.

"Come, I'll show you."

As we walked, there was a strange silence between us. When we reached his aunt's flat, he started climbing the steps.

I stood still.

"Are you coming?" His eyes were pleading.

"I don't know, Ben."

"Come on," he said, taking my hand and gently leading me up the steps.

As he opened the door, the flat was quiet. "Where's your aunt?" I asked. "She's always here."

"She's gone for a week . . . to help with a wedding."

"Really? Who's getting married? Someone I know?"

"It doesn't matter." His answer was short as he pushed the door shut with his foot. Then he held me tightly and kissed me more passionately than ever before.

I pushed him back.

"Are you afraid?" he asked, his voice full of loving concern.

"No . . . I mean, I don't know. I didn't expect *this*."

"Don't worry," he smiled, his face as confident as his voice.

We sat on the edge of the bed, and he began kissing me softly on my neck and ear. Then he moved to my lips. At first his kiss was light, but it grew stronger until our lips were pressed against our teeth. Then his mouth opened, and his tongue met mine. I didn't want to kiss like that. Gently I pushed him back so we could talk.

Before I could say anything, he whispered, "Let's have the new experience. Let's have it now."

"But Ben . . . ." I protested half-heartedly.

"Remember, it's just like ice cream." He waited quietly while thoughts raced through my mind.

I was afraid, yet I also felt excited about the idea of sex. I knew we loved each other. And it's true that it would have been a mistake to wait until I was 25 to try ice cream. Maybe sex is the same way. But why do adults try to keep sex from us? Do they have some good reason?

"Kiss me, Sweet Baby," he whispered.

His kisses became gentle again. I didn't push him back. All I wanted was to be near him. The outside world seemed to disappear as I entered a new world of closeness to Ben. As we kissed, our tongues found each other again. His hands were touching my body everywhere, and I didn't stop him. I didn't want to stop him. From head to toe I had a fantastic feeling of love. "Just once," I told myself. "Why should I wait? I'm sure I couldn't get pregnant the first time."

It didn't take us long to undress. I was surprised that my nakedness didn't embarrass me.

We got into bed, then . . . it hurt!

No one ever told me it would hurt. I had expected a feeling of highest pleasure.

When he finished, he kissed me once on the cheek. Then he rolled over and went to sleep.

I couldn't cry. Yet I felt very ashamed of myself.

I also felt surprised. Silently I asked, "Is that *it?* Is that the experience everyone says is so terrific?"

Slowly I got out of bed. I didn't want to waken Ben. I picked up my clothes and dressed. Then I just sat in a chair and watched him sleep. I didn't know what else to do. I couldn't even think.

3

Over an hour passed before Ben woke up. "Baby," he said cheerfully, "are you glad you tried it?"

I smiled weakly and told a lie, "Sure. It was great."

"Come over here," he motioned with his hand.

I sat on the edge of the bed, hoping he wouldn't touch me. He reached up and put his hand on my cheek. Then he pulled me down and kissed me gently. "He kisses sweetly, but doesn't care about my feelings," I thought angrily.

"Why did you put your clothes on?" he said while caressing my leg. "You were beautiful without them."

"Oh, am I not beautiful with clothes on?" I tried to keep my voice sweet. I didn't want to make Ben angry.

He sat up in bed, looking at me. "What's the matter, Sindie? Is something bothering you?"

"I'm sorry, Ben. It's . . ." I looked at my watch so I could tell another lie. "It's late. I must get home. Mother will wonder where I am."

I gave him a quick kiss on the cheek and hurried out the door.

On the way home I avoided all the main streets. I didn't want meet anyone who knows me. I just wanted to get home where I could be alone. And I desperately wanted to wash myself . . . to get *clean* again.

Quietly I went to my room and took off my clothes. I hid them under my bed until I could find a chance to wash them myself. I didn't want Mother to see them.

I stayed in my room until dinner time. I felt afraid to face my family. I was sure they would *know* just by looking at me.

But at dinner I realised: They didn't know . . . for them it's just another meal.

So I forced myself to smile and join them in talking about the usual things.

After dinner I was glad to be back in my room, away from the presence of my family. But sleep refused to come and save me from my rushing thoughts.

Each time I closed my eyes, I could feel Ben's body against mine. I could feel his motion . . . the motion that made me feel dirty.

"Why do I feel so guilty?" I kept asking myself.

The next time we had sex, Ben used a condom. "Don't worry, Sweet Baby," he said. "From now on, I will use a condom every time we make love."

The words "make love" hit me. I wondered: Is it really true that sex is "*making* love"?

For the rest of the week I gave Ben sex whenever he asked. Each time I hoped to feel the excitement . . . the excitement you always hear certain girls talking about. But every time I was disappointed again.

I did enjoy the romantic way he fondled me. Each time before sex, he kissed me passionately. His tender words always softened my heart. "Sindie, I love you, I love you," he kept repeating.

But all too soon he would enter me, and my pleasure would disappear.

One week…two weeks…three weeks slowly passed. I nearly forgot how to laugh. I grew quiet and angry.

One day Mom asked me, "Sindie, what's happening to you? You've changed. Where's my happy, cheerful girl?"

Mother was concerned about me, but Ben wasn't. He was so selfish. He just wanted sex to satisfy himself.

The phone rang. I picked it up and heard Ben's excited voice. "Hi, Sweet Baby. Can you meet me at Dan's?"

I wanted to refuse, but somehow I forced myself to act excited. "Sure, Ben, I'll see you in a few minutes."

Hanging up the phone, I thought, "What a great actress I've become! And how tired I feel of acting!"

As I slowly walked to meet him, I realised: I need to talk with someone about my situation. But who? I can't talk with Joy. I feel like I no longer know her.

"Sindie!"

In surprise I turned and saw Ruth walking behind me. "Ruth," I said nervously. "I haven't seen you for so long."

"I know," she smiled. "I've missed you. I also wanted to ask: Can you take care of Joel on Saturday?"

My mind was so mixed up, it took me a minute to realise she had asked a question. "Uh . . . yes," I finally answered. "It will be a pleasure."

"Sindie, is anything troubling you?" she looked into my eyes with concern.

"Not really." Thinking quickly, I knew I had to lie again. I wanted to talk with her, but I certainly didn't want her to know about Ben. So I just said, "Yesterday I heard that Priscilla had her baby. It's a girl."

"That's nice," Ruth smiled.

"Now," I continued, "she's not going back to school. Instead she's going to look for a job." I paused, trying to think of the right words for my next sentence. "Ruth, when I heard that Priscilla was pregnant, I started thinking about . . . sex. Now I need to ask you some questions. Can we talk some time?"

"Sure, Sindie. Do you mean today?"

"No, right now I'm going . . . somewhere."

"Okay," Ruth said. "How about tomorrow afternoon at my house?"

"Fine," I said, forcing a smile. Then I looked at my watch and said a quick good-bye.

The following day as I entered Ruth's house, little Joel came running to me. "Sindie, Sindie," he said in his sweet, childish voice.

Ruth poured us each a glass of juice and we sat down. After the usual small talk, she asked, "So, what questions are on your mind?"

Trying to keep my voice normal, I began, "Priscilla's pregnancy started me thinking." I breathed deeply, trying to push out the next words that were so heavy on my chest. "Ruth . . . do you like sex?"

Without much surprise in her voice she replied, "Yes, I love sex with my husband. Why do you ask?"

I tried to sound like I had little interest in the subject. "Magazines write so much about sex, and some girls talk about it. I just wanted to ask if sex is really so great. In our culture, most people don't talk about such things. You are the only one I could ask."

Ruth smiled understandingly. "Sindie, for many people sex is filled with guilt and fear. Why? Because they take sex outside of marriage. Listen, Sindie. The key to lovely sex is marriage — a marriage filled with trust and love. You see, I *trust* my husband. I don't fear that he will leave me. So, I don't give him sex to *keep* him. We just enjoy each other. During sex, he's not just thinking of himself. He cares about me and makes sex satisfying for me too. He unselfishly *loves* me."

Thoughts raced through my mind . . . finally I said, "But even without marriage, I think it's still possible to have 'trust' and 'love.'" As I said those words, I realised: I don't *trust* Ben's *love* for me. I always fear that if I refuse sex, he will leave me.

"Listen, Ruth," I continued, "the question I really want to ask is: How can sex before marriage be wrong?"

"Because," Ruth said simply, "God says it's wrong. And he has good reasons for saying so. He knows us well. He made us, and he made sex."

"What are his reasons?" I asked skeptically.

"One reason is sex-diseases. Did you know that people who live in sexual sin often catch **S**exually **T**ransmitted **D**iseases?"

"You mean HIV?"

"HIV is one of them. And there are more than a dozen others. For example, the disease 'gonorrhea' is spread by sex. It can make a person childless. In fact, my younger sister will never have a baby—just because she had sex with a boy who happened to have gonorrhea. How she wishes that she had said 'no' to sex before marriage!"

I let my face show concern, but said nothing.

Ruth picked up little Joel and gave him some juice. Then she continued, "God loves us. He wants each husband and wife to enjoy marriage and enjoy sex."

"Wait a minute," I interrupted. "On TV they say that God doesn't want anyone to enjoy sex."

Ruth laughed. "Just the opposite! God wants us to enjoy it. But we must realise this one thing: God designed *sex for marriage,* just like He designed *fish for water.* Fish belong in water, and sex belongs in marriage. So, people who have sex outside marriage don't find the true joy that God planned."

"But I've heard girls say that no one wants to marry a virgin. How can I be a good lover if I don't practise before marriage?"

Now little Joel was asleep and Ruth laid him down. "I realise many young people say that. But in fact, the *best* way to begin marriage is: *A virgin bride and a virgin groom.* Then after the wedding, she enjoys learning to satisfy her husband, and he enjoys learning to satisfy her. Neither of them is thinking, 'How do I compare with his/her previous sex-partners?' Instead, they start fresh."

I looked at the floor and asked, "Then, why do guys try so hard to get sex from girls before marriage?"

"Many guys are selfish. They think, 'Sex is fun for me.' So he gets on the girl, gets off, and tells himself, 'I enjoyed it — that's all that matters.' He doesn't really care about her."

Ruth shook her head and added, "How selfish!"

"I don't understand all this," I said, telling a lie. In fact, I understood that sex can be very selfish. I was experiencing it with Ben.

Ruth looked up at me. "Sindie, just understand this: God planned for sex to be a precious gift for each husband and wife to give each other. Sex is good. And God's law is good. I mean, his law that tells us to save sex for marriage."

"Were you still a virgin on your wedding day?" I asked rather boldly.

"Yes, both Simon and I were. *But it wasn't easy!* We succeeded only because God helped us, and we were careful to avoid bedrooms and bushes!" Ruth smiled, her eyes looking far away as she remembered it all. Then she turned her eyes to me and said, "Sindie, wait for sex. Wait until your wedding day. You'll be glad you did."

"Thanks for the talk," I tried to smile.

"Any time, Sindie. I'll see you on Saturday, I hope."

"Sure." I kissed Joel softly on the cheek and said "Bye."

As I was walking home, a car passed by with the radio blaring loudly:

> "You are my dream,
> my life, my love.
> I'll never leave you."

I could not stop my tears. Ruth was right about sex. I knew that I must stop hurting myself. I must tell Ben 'no.'

4

"Ben, I can't continue like this." I pressed my face against his naked chest.

His arms held me, and he pulled me close, "What do you mean, Sweet Baby?"

"I want to be . . ." his chest quickly became wet with my tears. "I want to be a girl again. I'm tired of acting like a wife. I don't want any more sex until the day I become a wife."

I hoped his reaction would be kind and understanding. Instead, he pushed me back so that he could look at my face.

"What do you mean?" he demanded angrily.

I just looked at him through tear-filled eyes.

"To me," he continued, "sex is fantastic. How can you *not* want it?"

Suddenly I understood him. I stopped crying as anger filled my heart and voice. "Now I see! You think I may tell someone that you are useless in bed. You don't care about me. You just fear that I may spoil your reputation."

I jumped out of bed, turned my back on him, and quickly put on my clothes. As I turned to leave, I noticed his eyes were narrow with anger. He remained silent as he watched me go.

On the way home I told myself, "I must just forget

Ben. I must go back to the life I was living before I ever met him."

When I reached the house, I walked past my sister without saying a word and went straight to the phone. I had nearly forgotten Joy's number.

"Hi, Joy," I tried to sound cheerful. "How are you? Can you go shopping with me today?"

She was silent. Then in a bitter voice she asked, "Where's Ben? Did he go back to Malesus?"

"No. But Joy...we haven't seen each other since ...."

Her voice softened. "Sindie, I'm glad you phoned. Honestly, I've been feeling hurt ... thinking that you no longer have time for me."

"I never wanted to hurt you, Joy. I've been so busy. But what I really want to say is ... I'm sorry."

"It's okay, Sindie. I'll meet you in town as usual."

"Thanks, Joy. I'll see you there. Bye."

After shopping we sat at Dan's sipping Cokes. I tried so hard not to cry, but then a tear slipped out. I waited until she was looking the other direction, then I quickly wiped my cheek.

But she caught me. "Sindie, what is it? You've not been yourself all day ... and now your eyes are watery. Please tell me what's bothering you."

I tried to speak, "Oh, Joy...." Tears poured down my cheeks. I had to grab my tissues and run out the door.

Looking over my shoulder, I saw her trying to follow me. I'll never forget the concerned look on her face as she tripped over chairs in her attempt to catch me.

"Sindie, *Sindie!*" her voice pleaded.

I continued running until I turned the corner. When I was sure she could no longer see me, I slowed to a walk and let my angry tears flow.

By the time I reached home, the tears had dried, but anger was still boiling inside me. On my bed I found a small note: *Ben phoned. Phone him back.*

It was written by my sister, Eunice. At age twelve she still writes so briefly—with no details.

My mind raced . . . maybe I should phone him and tell him how angry he makes me.

Just then the phone rang.

"Hello."

"Sindie, I'm sorry."

My voice was ice-cold. "Is that right?"

"I'm serious, Sindie. I'm sorry I made you angry. You know I love you."

The ice melted just a little.

"Do you forgive me?" he asked softly.

"I . . . guess so." Then the ice disappeared completely and I whispered, "I love you, too."

Ben was smart. He knew I needed to feel that someone loves me.

"Listen, Sindie. I understand what you said about sex. We can stop it for a week."

"Okay," I said, feeling a bit thankful. Probably he assumed I didn't want sex because of my period. But I wasn't having a period. I didn't even know when to expect my next period. I'm so irregular. Often I miss a period or two completely.

But I didn't say anything to Ben about periods. I was just glad for seven days of no sex.

So I enjoyed every minute of that week.

Ben and I walked and shopped together, and spent time listening to music. We also phoned his friends and met them for tennis. During the past month we hadn't been doing any of those things. How wonderful it was to talk, joke, and laugh again!

Sometimes in town we saw Joy. She always looked at me with concerned eyes, but I avoided speaking to her. I didn't want her to think that I was worrying about anything.

Then, the week was over.

Our first time back in bed showed me that nothing had changed there. I hid my disappointment from Ben. I wished I could talk with him about my feelings, but I knew he'd get angry again. So I just got out of bed, telling him I had to be home early.

At home, I walked straight to my room. I wanted to be alone so I could think about all my feelings. As I lay on my bed listening to *"You are my dream . . . ,"* I realised how confused my feelings were. They were up and down . . . loving Ben . . . not loving him. When Ben and I had our clothes on, my feelings were high and life was great. When our clothes were off, it was frustration and guilt.

I felt like shouting, *"I am not happy!"* But to whom could I shout it?

That's how the weeks passed.

Near the end of our summer holiday, Ben and I were sitting at Dan's. "Do you realise," I said, trying to be cheerful, "we are now sitting in the same place where we first met?"

Ben was strangely quiet.

I whispered, "Let's talk about the first time we met."

It seemed that Ben hadn't heard me. He just said, "I'm leaving tomorrow, Sweet Baby."

"Really? For how long?"

"Sindie, use your head! I'm going home. You know, back to Malesus. School opens Tuesday."

I had nearly forgotten that he would leave someday, permanently.

"Oh," was all I said. But why didn't I feel sad? Why wasn't I crying? Why did I feel like a heavy load would soon be lifted from me?

He touched my hand. "I don't know when I'll see you again, Baby."

"Won't I see you tomorrow?"

"No. I must leave early."

"Can't you visit me some weekends?"

"I don't know, Sindie. It's a long journey for a weekend. You know how expensive it is."

My feelings started going up and down again. One minute I was trying to think of ways for Ben to visit me. The next minute I was happy he couldn't.

Deep inside, I knew I shouldn't be having sex. I felt glad that it would soon end . . . and I could go back to being a school-girl again.

We left Dan's and walked as slowly as possible. When we neared my house, I turned to face him. "Ben, I . . . ."

Before I could say anything, he held my hand for a moment as he whispered, "I love you, Sindie. Goodbye."

He took a few steps, then looked back at me to say, "Don't forget our song."

Then, he just walked away.

It was so unlike all the romance books. Nothing fit — not my feelings, or his behaviour. I knew he was leaving tomorrow; yet it didn't seem possible that he would really go. He had become part of me.

As I walked home I told myself, "Love is strong. He will return in a few weeks. He won't be able to forget me."

5

This morning I made a terrible mistake. I laughed at the wrong time. Now I feel so ashamed. It happened when Ruth was saying something about Jesus. In the years I've known Ruth, often I've listened patiently to her talk about Him. It's obvious that Jesus is her best friend. Yet, she doesn't preach at you. She talks about Him naturally—the same way I talk about my friends.

It was after breakfast this morning when I went to visit her. She was sitting at her sewing machine making a dress. We talked as she sewed. Eventually I told her, "You know, sometimes I think no one loves me."

"Why's that, Sindie?" she asked while taking pins out of the half-finished dress.

"I don't know. Mom is so busy working. She has very little time to think of herself—or me."

"What about your dad?"

I thought for a moment. "Dad is always quiet. He seldom says anything to me, or to anyone. Mom says that his work makes him very tired, so he has no energy left when he gets home."

Ruth looked up from her sewing and said, "Sindie, in your heart you know they love you."

"Yes, I guess they do." I looked at the floor, avoiding her eyes. "I wish they would show it more often."

Then I looked up at Ruth and asked, "Why can't we always be loved?"

Ruth's kind eyes met mine. "Sindie, I have a friend who loves you all the time."

"Who?"

"Jesus."

That's when I laughed. I didn't mean to laugh, but her idea seemed so funny. *How could someone I don't even know... love me?*

Later, when I was home thinking about it, I told myself, "I must apologize to Ruth. But not today. I have too many other things to do. School opens tomorrow."

So, I pushed the whole 'apologize idea' to the back of my mind. The next morning I was full of smiles as I walked to school. Joy was waiting for me near her home. "Why so sad?" I asked cheerfully.

"The opening of school is the *worst* time of the year," she complained as we walked on together.

"No," I said. "The worst time is *Exam Week!"*

"Right!" she laughed. "How could I forget? I'll be so glad when I'm finished with school. Just think, only two more years!"

Our conversation flowed easily—just like the good days before the holiday—before Ben.

"What subjects did you choose?" she asked me.

"History, biology, and . . . ."

"*Biology!?"* Joy interrupted. "Why that? Mr Sanka teaches it. He's *so boring!"*

"But I must take biology. How will I pass science in university if I have no background?"

Soon the school was full of students, all excitedly asking each other, "How was your holiday?" Whenever anyone asked me, I just smiled weakly and said, "Fine."

Before our first class, Joy said to me, "After school today, come over to my house so we can have a good talk."

"Thanks Joy, but I've been so tired lately, I think I'll go straight home and rest."

"*Rest?* Are you serious?"

I felt embarrassed, and so I just hurried to class without saying anything more.

After school I told my sister, "If anyone phones, you can find me in my room." Then I went straight to bed and fell asleep while listening to "our" song.

"Sindie . . . Sindie, wake up!"

I opened my eyes and saw Mom shaking my foot. "Is it the phone?" I asked immediately.

"No, it's dinner time. Come, you Sleepy-head."

During the rest of the week, Mom always had to wake me for dinner. Then she would scold me because I hadn't helped with the cooking.

I felt bad for not helping her, but I was always too tired. I guess my new classes at school were taking all my energy.

Each evening as I studied biology, I flew to the phone every time it rang. I always said a warm "Hello," hoping to hear Ben's voice. But every time it was someone else, and my disappointment grew.

By Sunday I was filled with worry. Why didn't Ben phone?

Monday morning I forced myself out of bed only thirty minutes before I had to meet Joy. I felt so tired. Maybe it was because I got up twice during the night to go to the toilet.

Hurriedly, I ate breakfast and ran out of the house.

"I nearly gave up on you," Joy shouted before I reached her.

"Sorry," I said sleepily.

As we walked, Joy held my books while I put the belt on my uniform. "By the way," she said, "I've noticed how sick you always look during history class. Is that class too difficult for you?"

I took my books back from her as I replied, "No, the problem is: Every day during history class my stomach starts feeling strange, and I think I'm going to vomit. I don't know why. Maybe it's because history is just before lunch when my stomach is empty. I will be so embarrassed if I ever vomit right in class!

"Another thing I can't understand is: I get the same sick feeling when I try to eat fish. In fact, even if someone near me eats fish, I stand up and walk away. In the past I've always loved fish! But now . . . oh . . . just the thought of it makes me *sick*."

Joy made no comment on my food problems. Instead she asked the question I hoped she would never ask. "Has Ben phoned you?"

"Not yet," I admitted.

"I hate to see that useless guy break your heart," she said bitterly. "You can't trust guys. One minute they promise you eternal love . . . the next they forget you. *I wish you would just forget him!*"

I couldn't believe my best friend would talk to me like that. Probably she was jealous because I had spent so much time with Ben instead of her. I nearly threw hurtful words back at her, but I really didn't want to lose her friendship. So I didn't say another word. There was cold silence between us as we walked on to school.

After our first class, I gave her a smile as I turned to go to biology, and I knew we were still friends when her eyes lit up and she smiled back.

Half-way through biology, I began thinking about my

bladder. It was full . . . painfully full!

I tried to listen to Mr Sanka, but the painfull feeling kept growing.

"Does anyone here like school?" Mr Sanka asked loudly.

No one raised a hand.

"Now class, you must realise that you need education to meet the demands of the modern world."

I could not wait another minute. I raised my hand.

"Yes, Sindie. Do *you* see the value of education?"

"No . . . I mean, yes . . . but I want to ask: May I go out?"

Mr Sanka looked embarrassed, and students tried to hold back their laughter.

"Yes, Sindie, you are excused. Now class, let's . . . ." Mr Sanka's voice faded as I ran to the toilet.

I'm surprised that I can no longer get through two classes without a toilet-trip. I guess I must start going there before each and every class.

The other girls are beginning to notice my problem. They joke about it, saying things like, "Sindie, what are you drinking these days? You spend more time in the latrine than in class."

Even Joy jokes about it. I told her, "I'm having painful cramps, and so I expect my period to come soon."

It's true that cramps are a normal part of my monthly life as a 'woman.' But going to the toilet every hour — that's new. And my cramps are becoming more painful.

During break Joy asked me, "How's volleyball?"

"I love it. Our team wins every game!" Then I pulled Joy near as I whispered, "My only problem is: Some parts of my body are growing too fast. As I run and jump during the game, my breasts hurt with every shake."

"Be happy your boobs are big enough to shake," she whispered. "Look at me. My chest still looks more like my father's than my mother's."

"Thanks a lot!" I said as we both laughed.

That afternoon I had just gone to sleep when my sister shook my arm and said, "Phone." Then she turned and walked off.

Trying to wake up my sleepy brain, I slowly walked to the phone. "Hello."

"Hi, Sweet Baby. What's up? Your voice sounds like you've had a hard day."

"Yes, I mean, no. I've been asleep."

"Asleep! In the middle of the day?"

"Ya, recently I feel tired all the time," I yawned. "I don't know why."

"Do you study at night and go to bed late?"

"No . . . that's why I don't understand it."

Now I was fully awake and I remembered to ask, "Why didn't you phone sooner?"

"Baby, you know how busy the first week of school is."

"I'm sorry your week was too busy for me." I allowed him to see my hurt feelings.

"You seem bitter today," he said softly. "Where's my cheerful, *Sweet* Baby?"

I smiled as I listened to his smooth voice. Ben always knew how to melt my anger and fears.

Then he said, "Now tell me straight. How's school?"

"It's okay, except biology." Then I had to ask, "When will I see you again?"

He was silent for a long time. I knew I had asked the wrong question. Then in an impatient voice, he replied, "I don't know. . . ."

I tried again, "Ben, I miss you . . . a lot."

"Okay . . . I'll phone you on Friday. Bye."

"Ben, I . . . ." but he had already put down the receiver. His attitude confused me. Now I felt even more empty than before he phoned.

I returned to my room and sat on the bed. Crying didn't help much, but I couldn't stop myself.

Then the phone rang again. I ran to answer it, hoping he had decided to phone back. *"Hello,"* I said in my most cheerful voice.

"Hi, Sindie. Why are you so happy?" It was Ruth. I felt so disappointed, I began to cry.

"What's wrong, Sindie?" her voice was filled with love as always.

"Someone special phoned."

"That should make you happy."

"I know. But it didn't. I feel terrible."

"I'm sorry, Sindie. Would you like to come over here so we can talk about it?"

"No thanks. Don't worry, I'll be fine."

"Okay, Sindie. Listen, I'm phoning to ask if you can care for Joel on Saturday evening."

"But aren't you angry at me?"

"For what?"

"For the way I laughed when you talked about Jesus."

"Of course not, Sindie."

"I want to apologize . . . ."

"That's not necessary. Can you come on Saturday? My husband is taking me to the Continental for dinner."

"Oooh how nice! Yes, I'll be happy to come."

"Thanks, Sindie. But are you sure you're okay?" her voice showed real concern.

"Oh, I don't know. I've been feeling so unusual recently." Then my words began to pour quickly out.

"I sleep a lot, and have pain like I'm going to start my period. I eat more than usual, but I can't eat fish. I go to the toilet often. Every day I feel sick during history class. I cry one minute, laugh the next, and have headaches."

For the first time I had put all my new feelings together. Suddenly, I wished I could push the words back into my mouth. Why did I tell all this to Ruth?

When I stopped talking, she was silent for a long, long time. I thought she may have left the phone. "Hello, Ruth . . . ?"

Her voice was soft. "Oh Sindie, I think you may be pregnant."

"But, I can't be." I was shocked! "To be pregnant, you must have a big stomach. And you must have sex to get pregnant," I said in my most innocent voice. "No, I'm sure my period will start tomorrow."

I didn't want her to ask any questions. So I quickly said, "I'll see you Saturday. Bye."

Standing in front of my mirror, I pulled up my shirt and looked at my stomach — front and side views. Nothing seemed different. I couldn't be!

But my period was a *long* time ago. When did I have my last one? It was . . . the end of November.

Then I began to think. This is *February! It's been over eight weeks!*

I gasped with surprise, and let my shirt fall. Trying not to cry, I whispered Ruth's words, *"Oh Sindie, I think you may be pregnant."*

6

Sometimes I hate the night. At night every worry grows. As I try to fall asleep, I can't get comfortable. I flip-flop like a fish out of water. Then I try to lie very still, but my mind refuses to be quiet. Finally I fall asleep, and when I open my eyes, it's morning!

The bright sun chases away all my worries. Of course I'm not pregnant. If I were pregnant, certainly I would know it.

During the next two days I forgot my fears and felt especially cheerful, although my body continued its unusual behaviour.

I remembered that Ben promised to phone on Friday, and I eagerly looked forward to hearing his voice. "This time," I told myself, "I will not say anything about his coming to see me," although my heart was dying to see him!

Friday afternoon he phoned, just as he had promised. What a darling! We talked about his school and mine. Then my heart made me say, "I miss your touch, Ben."

"Ya, Sweet Baby, I miss your touch, too." His voice was soft and romantic.

How I wanted him to hold me and kiss me! I was quiet so long that he asked, "Are you still there, Baby?"

"Yes, Sweetheart," I replied slowly, "I'm still here. But I wish I were there—with you."

"I feel the same way, Baby." Then he added, "Listen to our song and think of me, okay? Bye."

After listening to *"I'll Never Leave You"* three times, I floated into the kitchen. Mom's eyes were wide with surprise as I started helping before she even called me. Yet, she asked no questions and I said nothing. I didn't want anything to break my bubble of joy.

As I put plates on the table, I was quietly singing, "I'll never leave you. I love you today and forever...."

When my sister entered the room and heard me singing, she rolled her eyes and said, "I'm so *sick* of that song!"

I just smiled and continued singing, "I'll always be near. I'll never leave you...."

During dinner the wonderful song continued in my heart. I felt happy as I sat at the table with my parents, brother and sister. I enjoyed listening as everyone talked about their day. I was on a cloud. Nothing could spoil my joy.

"This food is delicious, Mom," I said cheerfully as I dished more rice onto my plate.

Suddenly everyone became quiet.

I looked up to see the reason for the silence. Everyone was staring at *me!*

"Why are you all looking at me?"

"We're surprised to see you eating so much," Mom said.

"This isn't 'so much.'"

"It's your second plate full."

"What's wrong with that? Luke always fills his plate twice."

"Yes, but your brother is a growing boy. He needs to eat a lot."

"If boys can eat a lot, why not girls?"

Dad finally spoke. "Let's not over-do this. Sindie, we are just surprised because you normally eat very little, but now you are eating more. That's all."

Mom added, "If you continue like this, you will need new clothes two sizes larger."

Fortunately they were only worried that I may grow *fat*. They didn't suspect pregnancy. But their remarks started my mind working again. In fact, my clothes were beginning to feel tight . . . for what reason?

I put down my fork. I no longer felt hungry. Fear filled my stomach. I knew that I *must* find out whether I'm pregnant or not. Slowly my mind made a plan.

"Mom, do you still remember that I'm going to Ruth's home Saturday evening?"

"I've not forgotten. And don't you forget that you must clean the house before you go."

"Is it okay if I do the cleaning after lunch? I'd like to spend the morning at the library. . . studying."

"Okay, Sindie. Just be sure you're home by noon."

I nodded and began taking dishes to the kitchen.

Fear held me night and day for the rest of the week. Finally Saturday came. As I walked to the library, I desperately hoped to find my answer there.

I soon found a shelf of books on pregnancy. Then I carefully looked around to be sure no one was watching me.

"May I help you?" a voice surprised me from behind.

It was the librarian! I wondered if she could hear my heart pounding as I said, "No thanks . . . I've found what I'm looking for." I pointed to some biology books.

She nodded and walked away.

I waited until she sat at her desk. Then I opened a

large book entitled Pregnancy. It had a chapter on symptoms, but the only things it mentioned were "softening of the uterus" and "increased blood supply."

Rubbish! Too scientific! I don't care about my uterus or blood. I only want to know if I'm pregnant.

The second book was equally large. One chapter looked promising: "Are You Pregnant?" As I read, people often walked near me, and I had to hide the book under my jersey. This book was also useless—full of big words that I couldn't understand.

After two hours I decided to give up. There must be a better way to find the answer.

That afternoon, Mom was happy with the way I cleaned the house. I worked hard and fast, trying to keep my mind from thinking about the awful question.

Later the question followed me to Ruth's house. As she greeted me, her eyes showed both love and worry. She said nothing about our phone conversation, but I knew she understood the question on my mind.

As she and Simon were leaving, she looked at me and said, "You are free to look at any of my books. Perhaps you'll find something interesting."

Our eyes met in silent understanding. "Thanks," I said sincerely.

I put Joel to bed a bit early, then I went straight to the book shelf. Two titles looked hopeful. I began reading them, but neither one helped me.

Discouragement flooded my heart as I replaced them on the shelf. Both spoke only of morning sickness and constipation. I don't have *those* symptoms. So what about *me?* Am I pregnant?

I looked doubtfully at the shelf again. I picked one entitled, Family Medical Book and opened it to "Chapter 9 . . . Pregnancy."

There my eyes fell on the words, "A Family Planning Clinic will give a free pregnancy test to anyone."

Perfect! That's it! That's exactly what I need!

I grabbed Ruth's telephone directory. Flipping through the pages I soon found, "Family Planning Clinic." I wrote the number on a piece of paper and put it in my pocket.

Looking at the address, I was surprised to find that this clinic was near the library. I must have walked past it many times, but I couldn't remember ever seeing it.

As Ruth drove me home, we didn't talk much. When we stopped in front of my house, her words were warm and loving. "Sindie, no matter what happens, I'll always be your friend." I looked the other direction as she continued, "And Jesus hopes that you will accept Him as your friend."

"Thanks," I said, as if I knew what she was talking about. "Good-bye."

Monday morning passed so slowly. I couldn't smile. I felt sorry for Joy. She kept trying to cheer me up, but often I didn't even hear what she was saying. I just nodded my head to make her think I was listening.

After school I walked for a long time until I found a public phone that didn't have people standing near it. With shaking fingers I dialed the number.

"Family Planning," a friendly female voice answered.

"Hello, I need a . . . uh . . . pregnancy test."

Her voice remained cheerful. "Okay. Can you come tomorrow morning at 08:30?"

"Yes."

"Bring with you a small sample of your first morning urine."

"Uh . . . what shall I put it in?"

"Use a small, clean bottle. So, we will see you in the morning?"

"Yes. Good-bye."

Fear held me even more tightly as I reluctantly walked home.

7

Mom never throws away any bottle. I went to the box under the kitchen sink where she keeps them, and chose a small one. When no one was looking, I carefully washed it and hid it in my underwear drawer.

The next morning I woke up early and hurried to the toilet so I could secretly pass urine into the bottle.

I hadn't thought about how to carry it to the clinic. I didn't want it in my school bag — it might leak. Urine is not a nice perfume!

Finally I decided to put the bottle into two plastic bags, and then a brown paper bag.

Before Mother left for work, I went to her with my face twisted like I was in real pain. "Mom, I have period pains," I lied. "I don't think I can go to school until later in the morning. Can you please write a note and send it to school with Eunice?"

She looked at me. "Yes, okay."

Then she took a pill from her purse and handed it to me. "If you don't feel better soon, take this."

"Thanks," I said in a painful voice. "Good-bye."

I walked slowly to my bedroom and laid on my bed, just in case she decided to check on me before leaving for work.

When I heard her leave, I jumped out of bed, washed, and dressed. My radio was on, and suddenly a familiar song filled the room. *"I'll always be near. I'll never leave you."*

My heart jumped. Running to the radio, I switched it off as though it were sending poison into the room.

I took my brown bag and walked quickly to town. When I arrived at the place where I expected to find the clinic, the only thing I saw was a small sign reading, ***Family Planning Clinic*** and an arrow pointing to a passage between two buildings. Then I understood why I'd never noticed this clinic before. Walking that direction, I found the door and stepped inside.

The room was large with posters on every wall. On one side was a secretary sitting at a desk. On the other side was a circle of chairs. Two sad-looking girls of about my age were sitting there.

After the secretary wrote down my name, she told me, "Please sit over there until we call your name."

I thanked her and chose a chair far from the other girls. As I sat down, I slowly put my brown bag on the floor, hoping no one would see it.

Looking at the girl on my right, I noticed she was pretty and wearing a very expensive dress. She also looked very afraid. She sat with legs crossed and one foot bouncing up and down nervously.

I felt hot and fanned myself with a magazine.

Then I glanced at the girl on my left. She sat with her head down, staring at the floor and pulling her jersey tightly around her shaking body.

How could anyone feel cold in this hot room? Then

I noticed that *my* foot was bouncing nervously up and down.

A door opened and a lady in a blue uniform entered the room and called a name. The girl to my right picked up the brown bag under her chair and followed her, walking slowly with her head down.

After about ten minutes the same girl returned. What a change! She now had a bright smile as she walked lightly across the room and out the door.

The blue uniformed lady called another name. The cold girl jumped up, accidently dropping her brown bag. Quickly she picked it up and walked across the room. She looked even more fearful than the first girl.

While I was still waiting, the front door opened. Two women entered and were told by the secretary to take seats. They sat together and whispered—with quick glances at me—probably discussing how young I was.

Soon the inner door opened again, and this time a different lady in blue appeared. Her face was dark brown and she was very pretty. She looked at a card in her hand and said, "Sindie."

I picked up my bag and tried to walk with confidence. As I followed her, we passed the other girl; the cold one. Now her eyes were full of tears, and she was entering a door marked, "Counselling."

The pretty lady led me to her office. With a friendly smile she said, "I'm glad to meet you, Sindie. My name's Martha. Did you bring something for us?"

I nodded and handed her my bag. "Good," she smiled again. "Let's sit down."

Martha's office was nice and tidy. She sat at a metal desk and pointed me to a blue plastic chair in front of it. Then she picked up a pen and paper while saying, "Now Sindie, before I do the test I must ask you some questions. Everything you say in this office is a secret between me and you. So, don't be afraid to talk. And be sure to tell me the truth, okay?"

I nodded again, realising I had not yet said a word.

"How old are you?"

"Sixteen."

"When was your last period?"

"About the 28th of November."

"Did you use anything to prevent pregnancy—I mean condoms, or any other kind of Family Planning?"

"No, not the first time. But after that he began using condoms."

After writing a few words she looked up at me. "Sindie, why did you have sex that first time without using a condom?"

I thought I could never tell anyone how I had sex. I hadn't even told Joy. But this lady talked about sex as easily as other people discuss the weather. I took a deep breath and let the words rush out. "My periods are not regular. Sometimes I don't have a period for two or three months. So I thought I couldn't get pregnant easily—certainly not the *first* time. And then he started using condoms. Don't they prevent pregnancy?"

"Sindie, my child, a girl can get pregnant the *first* time she has sex—even if her periods aren't regular. In fact, a girl of age 12 (who has not yet had her first period) can get pregnant."

She paused a few seconds, probably to give me a chance to think about what she had said. Then she added, "About condoms—they do *help* to prevent pregnancy. Your boyfriend should have used one the first time and every time. However, sometimes a girl gets pregnant even when her boyfriend uses condoms."

I wanted to ask how that was possible, but I couldn't

force myself to speak about such things.

Martha leaned back in her chair and looked at me. "A school girl should not need condoms. School girls should just say 'no' to sex. But if a girl decides to have sex, she really must be sure that he wears a condom every time. He must put it on correctly, leaving space at the end. Then, soon after he ejaculates, he must remove the condom carefully, without spilling."

I looked down at my feet and said softly, "I will never again have sex until the day I marry."

"That's good! But my job at this clinic is to tell every girl, 'If you have sex, use a condom.' Yet I must say: Sindie, I'm glad you've decided not to have sex again until you marry. If you stick to that decision, you will avoid terrible sex-diseases, and your marriage will be brighter."

"Now let's do the test," she said as her eyes moved to my brown bag.

I nodded and watched as she took a test tube and a tiny bottle from the shelf behind her. Then she opened my bag and smiled as she noticed two plastic bags around my urine-bottle.

She put just five drops of my urine into the test tube. Then she added a drop of milky white liquid from her tiny bottle.

"What is supposed to happen?" I whispered.

"If you're not pregnant, this mixture will turn red. But if you are pregnant, it will remain white. Why? Because a pregnant lady always has the hormone HCG in her urine, and the HCG will make this mixture white."

"How long must we wait?"

"Only one minute."

I rubbed my sweaty hands together as we both stared at the clock.

When the minute was finally up, I looked at Martha. I was afraid to look at the test tube.

"Sindie," she said as she held the test tube to the light, "you are definitely pregnant."

I caught my breath and looked. The mixture was white. Nothing red anywhere.

Martha's voice was soft and understanding. "Sindie, it's important to tell your family immediately. Have you thought about that?"

"No . . . I mean, I never thought I really could be . . . ." I looked at her helplessly.

"I understand," she said sadly. "I see it every day. No girl thinks it can happen to her. And even now it may be difficult for you to believe it. But listen, Sindie. You *are* pregnant."

She paused, waiting for me to speak. But what could I say? Her test tube had just proved my deepest fear to be true.

Looking at me with eyes that were very serious, she said, "Sindie, don't even think of abortion. You do *not* want to kill your baby."

As she continued talking, I tried to listen, but I failed to concentrate on anything she was saying. It seemed to me that I was in the middle of a terrible dream. Oh, if only I could wake up and find that this whole pregnancy thing was just a bad dream!

Martha stood and walked with me to the door. "Sindie," she said, "there is a good, Christian lady who comes here every day to counsel girls. She's a wonderful person. She quit her job just so she can spend more time helping girls. Would you like to meet her?"

"Not today," I said shaking my head. I couldn't say anything more without bursting into tears. I just wanted to get out of that clinic and into the real world again.

On my way passed the circle of chairs, two girls looked at me, studying my face. I turned my head and walked quickly past them.

Outside the bright sun hurt my eyes. I knew I must hurry home and change quickly into my uniform.

When I arrived at school, I had to enter biology class late, with all eyes on me. Mr Sanka looked impatient as he motioned for me to sit at my desk.

All day I felt like I was living in a different world. I felt cold, but the sun was bright and warm.

Joy kept asking why I arrived at school so late. Finally I said, "I woke up with period pains. I hope you didn't wait for me very long."

"No," she answered sadly. Her voice showed that she didn't believe my lies. Yet I was thankful that she asked no more questions.

That night I dropped into bed and let my tears flow — the tears I had been holding back all day.

I just wanted to sleep, and I didn't care if I never woke up.

8

As the sun rises, I'm telling myself: I don't want to be pregnant. A baby will certainly hurt my education and my future. I need to talk to Ben!

But each time I pick up the phone, my heart beats so fast I can't speak. Even if I could speak, what would I say? I don't know how to tell him.

So I wait for him to phone me. And as I wait, my mind plans how to tell him in a nice, gentle way that he's a father.

In my mind I picture him giving me a perfect answer to the problem. But I cannot imagine what answer that could be.

I know that I'll do whatever he tells me. I really want to please him.

I'm sure he will come here, kiss me and say, "There's nothing to worry about because I love you." Then, together we will tell my parents.

Finally, after four long days of waiting . . .

"Hi, Sweet Baby. How's life?"

"Why didn't you phone sooner? It's been nearly a week!" I was surprised by the bitterness in my voice. The days of fear and worry had made it impossible for me to be gentle like I had planned.

"Sorry, Baby," Ben said lightly. "I've been busy making decisions about my future. This is my last year of school. So I must think about which university I should attend, and if I should join the soccer team . . . ."

How I tried to keep the anger out of my voice as I said, "You have one more decision to make about your future."

"What's that, Sweet Baby?"

Then my anger changed to tears. The hot tears poured down my cheeks. "Ben," I sobbed. "Oh, Ben . . . ."

"Stop crying, Sindie, and tell me what it is. This phone call is expensive!" His voice was so impatient. Where was the loving concern I had imagined?

Again I tried to say it. "Ben, I'm . . . pregnant."

He was quiet for a long moment. Then, *"You're what?"*

"You heard me," I said softly.

"Unfortunately!" His voice was ice cold.

"What are you going to do about it?" I asked.

"Listen, Sindie. Don't ask me what I'm going to do. It's *your* problem — not mine. I'm not pregnant. You are! And I don't know if the child is mine, or some other guy's."

No words could have hurt me more.

"It's yours," I kept my voice soft. "I'm about two months pregnant." I nearly broke into tears again, but stopped myself.

Ben became gentle. "I'm sorry, Sweet Baby. Of course it's mine. You just surprised me, that's all."

I decided to ask my question again, desperately hoping he had an answer. "So Ben . . . what do we do?"

"There's only one answer. Get rid of it!"

"You mean, abortion?"

"Yes, of course."

"Wait a minute, Ben. I don't feel right about abortion. Last year a girl I know gave herself an abortion. I was so angry with her . . . I just wanted to slap her face and shout, 'Lydia, how could you kill your baby?'"

"Listen, Sindie, you have no other choice. We don't want a kid."

The words cut deep into my heart. Sadly I answered, "Okay Ben, if you say so. But what will our families say?"

"We will never tell them? Listen to me. That girl you mentioned . . . Lydia . . . she can show you how to do it."

He sounded so business-like. I felt I must ask him, "Ben, do you love me?"

With *no* romance in his voice he replied, "That's a foolish question. Yes, I love you."

"Will you come see me soon?"

"I'll try."

"You don't sound very promising."

"How can I *promise?* Travelling such a distance by bus is no joke."

"Yes, Ben, I know. But I really need to see you."

"Look, I must go now. Bye."

I had neither the words nor the strength to protest. I put down the phone and went to my room. There I sat on my chair, looking at the floor. I couldn't even cry. I was too confused.

9

It was Friday before I forced myself to speak to Lydia. Even though she and I are on the same volleyball team, we don't know each other well. She's two years older than me.

Our team had just finished a game when I whispered to her, "Lydia, I need your help. Can we go to my classroom and talk? No one will see us there."

She noticed how fearful I was, and so she lowered her voice to a whisper, "Sure, Sindie. Let's go."

We entered the classroom and chose desks in the back, away from the windows. Lydia is so tall and her hips so big, the school desk seemed much too small for her.

I was looking down at the floor as I shoved out the awful words, "Lydia, I need an abortion."

"How far along are you?" her voice remained calm.

"Two months."

"Does your boyfriend know?"

"Yes."

"What's he say?"

"He's the one who suggested abortion."

"Of course. Boys always do."

I didn't like the way she talked about my Ben. "He loves me and wants what is best for me," I said sharply.

"Is that right? If he loves you so much, why doesn't he keep your child and marry you?"

Her voice was making a joke of it. Oh, how could she joke about such things? I wanted to defend Ben, but I couldn't think of any good reply.

Lydia touched my hand and said, "Sindie, I'm not trying to find fault with your guy. Maybe he's different than the one who made me pregnant. But, I'm surprised that abortion wasn't *your* idea. I mean, why didn't you think of it first?"

"Me? . . . I've never liked the thought of abortion."

"Then why are you going to do it?"

"Because," I said slowly, "my boyfriend told me to."

Suddenly, a million thoughts raced through my mind. Whose idea is this abortion? It's Ben's. It's *only* Ben's — not mine. I haven't even thought about it. I can't think about anything. My mind is too mixed up.

Lydia looked at me sadly, remembering the time when she was going through all this herself. Gently she said, "On Monday I can bring you the medicine you need."

"Will it hurt?" I whispered.

"Not much. It feels like period-pains."

"Will I bleed?"

"I had trouble with bleeding for a few days — then it stopped."

I knew that Lydia was trying to encourage me, but as she talked, I was growing more and more fearful.

"How much money should I bring?" I just wanted to end this matter and go *home!*

"It used to be expensive, but I know a place where I

may get it cheaper. Phone me on Sunday afternoon and I'll tell you." She took a pen and wrote her number on a scrap of paper. As she handed it to me, she added, "Don't worry, Sindie, I'll never tell anyone. And you keep your mouth shut. I don't want to get into trouble!"

"Thanks for your help," I tried to smile.

As I walked home, the sun was still shining, but its warmth failed to reach my shaking insides. I had to keep wiping my eyes. I walked with my head down so that no one could see my face. Oh, how I wished to die—before Monday!

* * * * * * *

Here I sit in church with Mom and Dad. I hate church. No one in this church is friendly to me. And the preaching is always dry. Usually I just think about other things. But today I don't want to think. I'm so tired of the same thoughts rushing through my mind.

Can I really do it? Can I kill my baby?

But I must! I cannot tell my family that I'm pregnant!

Will the medicine harm my body? Will my baby feel pain? Will he feel himself *dying?*

I must never tell anyone. No one must know—not even joy. Only Ben.

And Ruth? No, I must never tell her. I'll let her think she was wrong about my being pregnant.

As I thought about Ruth, I noticed a mother sitting to my left. A little boy was sleeping in her arms. He was about the same age as Ruth's little Joel. He looked so peaceful! What joy a child brings to his mother!

And can I kill mine?

Even after I marry, perhaps I will never succeed in becoming pregnant. Who knows . . . this may be the only child I'll ever have!

Oh, I can't do it! I just cannot! But what other way is there? *I'm so confused! Who can I turn to? I need Ben! Oh, how I need Ben!!!*

10

"Forget it, Sindie. Our relationship is over."

"But, Ben . . ." I begged through my tears.

"Sindie, tell me straight. Did you really tell Lydia that you no longer want an abortion?"

"Yes, Ben, but please listen. I . . . ."

"Look, Baby. You really make me angry! I told you to get an abortion. But you don't do what I tell you. So we must just forget each other.

"But Ben, I love you. And I thought you loved me."

"I *thought* I loved you. You *thought* you loved me. We were both mistaken. It wasn't real love."

"Ben, I need your help."

"Okay, I'll send you some money."

"Not only that kind of help. Ben, I need *you*."

"Sindie, I'm telling you 'no.' To me, you were a pretty girl; but now you are becoming a problem. I want my life to go on without problems."

"What about *my* life, Ben?" I shouted angrily. "Do you think I'll have no problems? Haven't you created problems for me?"

"Listen, Baby. Your problems are *your* problems. And I'm never going to admit to my parents or to your parents that I'm the father of your baby. In fact, I don't want to hear from you again—ever! *Understand?*"

"No, I do *not* understand! You *will* hear from me! Good-bye!" I slammed down the receiver as hard as I could; just to be sure he knew how furious I was.

I felt so hurt and confused. Why must my life be so rotten?

When my tears finally stopped, I felt like a lion caught in a trap. My energy was ready to explode. I needed to talk to someone . . . someone who loved me.

I picked up the phone and dialed Ruth's number. It rang again and again . . . no answer.

I dialed another number. "Hi, Joy. It's me. I really need to talk to you . . . ." I broke into tears again.

"Sindie, what's the matter?" her voice was soft.

"It's Ben. He just phoned and told me to forget him." My crying made it difficult to get the words out.

Slowly Joy said, "Sindie, that's not so bad. Honestly, I never thought Ben was a good guy for you."

"Please don't say that, Joy. There's something you don't know. But do you promise not to tell anyone?"

"You know I never tell our secrets."

"Listen, Joy. I'm . . . pregnant! Ben's the father!"

I could hear her struggle to catch her breath. Finally she asked, "Does Ben know?"

"Yes. He says that he never wants to see me again."

"Oh," was all she could say. The phone was quiet a long time. Then in a shaky voice she said, "Sindie, my mother needs help with dinner. I'll phone you later."

A big help she was! Where are my friends when I need them? Now who can I turn to? Who can save me from falling to pieces?

Rushing to my room, I slammed the door and fell on my bed face down.

I heard the phone ring, but I didn't move. I had no desire to speak to anyone. Soon my sister was knocking on my door and shouting, "Ruth's on the phone."

"I don't want to talk to her."

"So, what must I tell her?"

"I don't care."

Suddenly, I changed my mind. Running to the phone, I grabbed the receiver before Eunice reached it. Then I gave her a quick smile just to say, 'sorry.'

"Hello, Ruth," I said as cheerfully as possible.

"Hi, Sindie," Ruth said pleasantly. "I just want to ask how you're feeling."

I didn't want her to ask any questions, so I asked one myself. "Ruth, why can't my life be like yours?"

"What do you mean, Sindie?"

"I mean, why don't you fall to pieces when terrible things happen to you?"

"Sindie, you've seen me cry many times."

"But your tears are different from mine. You always say that something good will come out of the trouble. Even when you cry, you remain hopeful."

"Several years ago I wasn't very hopeful."

"So, what happened to change you?" I asked, trying to find the answer to my world of problems.

"It's Jesus. Since I took Him, I still have problems, but He gives me hope . . . ."

"Oh why can't you ever talk without bringing *Him* into it?" My words were bitter, but I didn't feel sorry.

"I can't stop talking about Jesus. He's my friend."

"If your Jesus is so great, why am I pregnant?" I closed my eyes, sorry I had opened my big mouth. Why did I tell her? She's such a good person. Now she's going to think I'm an awful sinner. She will no longer want me as a friend.

Then Ruth's loving voice made me feel warmer than I had felt in days. "I'm sorry you're in trouble, Sindie. Have you told your mother yet?"

"No."

"You should tell her soon."

"Why? What can she do?" I asked sourly.

"Mothers can be very helpful at a time like this," her voice was still gentle.

"I don't need help," I said, trying to sound confident.

"Sindie, please come and talk with me here at home. Come now. We can talk much better face to face."

I had no energy to talk to anyone. I just wanted to go to bed and forget everything. "Maybe another day, Ruth. Today I don't feel . . . ."

"Okay, Sindie. Just remember, I'm always here to listen, or advise, or whatever you need."

"Thanks," I said, really meaning it.

"And I'll be praying for you," she added.

What good will that do? I wanted to say. Yet, when I thought that maybe God actually cares how my heart is breaking, somehow I felt a little better.

After saying "Bye," I went straight to my room and forced my mind to think. Yes, I must tell Mom soon. It will hurt her. But I must tell her so that she can tell Dad. I could never tell him.

I wish I had a book entitled, *"How to Tell your Mother you are Pregnant."*

* * * * * * *

It's not easy to talk to Mom. She's so busy. When she isn't at work, she's cleaning the house. Each time I go near her, she sends me to clean some other room.

Several days passed while I tried to find the right time and the right words.

Finally, I realised: I cannot wait any longer . . . my fear keeps growing every day . . . I ***must*** tell yer today!

Mom was wearing a red cloth tied around her head, like she always does when cleaning. As she entered the sitting room, I could see that her mind was running through her list of things-to-do. I stepped in front of her. "Mom, I need to talk to you. It's important."

"Okay, Sindie," she said as she handed me a feather duster. "Let's sit down for tea after we get this house clean. Go and dust the bedrooms while I clean here. I won't forget the tea."

Gently she pushed me aside as I said with disappointment. "Yes, Mom."

I knew that when the house was clean, it would be time to cook. And after dinner, she and Dad were going to visit Dad's brother. They would return home late.

That evening I spent three long hours waiting for them to come home. To keep my mind busy, I finished all my school-work. When they finally arrived, Dad said his usual, "Good night," as he walked past me to their bedroom. As Mom passed, I took her hand and begged, "Please, Mom, can we talk now?"

For the first time she realised I was deeply troubled. She sat down, and I rubbed my sweaty hands together.

"Mom, do you remember when you said that I was over-eating and I would grow fat?"

As usual, she jumped to conclusions. "Oh, Sindie, did that hurt your feelings? You aren't really overweight."

"Mother, you don't understand. I *am* gaining weight. But it's not that I over-eat. It's because . . . I'm *pregnant*."

First *surprise,* and then *doubt* crossed her face. She looked at me from head to toe, searching for proof. As tears filled my eyes, she realised I was not joking.

Looking straight at me, she asked, "Sindie, are you sure? Have you had a pregnancy test at a clinic?"

"Yes, Mom."

She burst into tears, putting her head in her hands. "Sindie, how could you do this to me?" she sobbed.

"Mother," I pulled her hands from her face. "Please don't cry," I begged as my own tears blurred my vision.

Without another word, she turned and ran to her bedroom.

I sat there, wondering if my heart was still beating. I couldn't think. I felt dead inside. Ten minutes passed before I forced myself to stand up.

As I entered my room, I stood looking in my mirror. All of this must be happening to someone else — not me. The person in the mirror looking so fearful couldn't possibly be me.

Scalding hot tears ran down my cheeks.

I could hear soft crying and whispered voices coming from my parents' room. I got into bed and pulled my pillow tightly over my ears. I tried hard not to cry. Then a new fear grew inside me — the fear that tomorrow would come.

11

I awoke in the morning as Mother sat on my bed. Touching my shoulder, she said softly, "Sindie, I'm ready to talk to you now."

I opened my eyes, afraid of what she was going to say.

"Sindie, I couldn't talk to you last night. I needed time to think. I hope now I can tell you everything I want to say." Her hand moved from my shoulder to grab another tissue. "Really, I never thought I would be talking with you about something like this."

Suddenly Mom looked very old, with disappointment written all over her face. I looked away, ashamed.

"Honestly, I feel angry. Sindie, you turned your back on everything your aunt and I taught you about keeping yourself pure until marriage."

I felt like I was standing naked in front of her. She was obviously very embarrassed and that made me even more ashamed.

"Last night," she continued with difficulty, "as I kept thinking about all this, I blamed myself. I thought of many mistakes I made as a mother."

Suddenly I felt hopeful. *Maybe this isn't my fault.*

"But the truth is," Mom's voice turned sharp, "it's not *my* fault. You knew that the right time to begin sex is on your wedding night. But you chose to do wrong. It was your choice — not mine."

Tears filled my eyes as I said, "But, Mom . . . ."

She continued as though I had said nothing. "Of course, I blame the boy, too. Do you know which boy is responsible?"

"Yes."

"Are you 100% sure?"

I looked up at her, hurt that she would think that I had been sleeping with more than one boy. "Of course, he's the only boy I ever . . . ."

Mom touched my mouth to stop me from finishing my sentence. Then she continued, "Last night I began telling myself, *'It must be the boy's fault. He forced my daughter.'* "

"No, Mom, he didn't *force* me."

"I understand," she said slowly. Then, wiping her eyes, she added, "Sindie, now your father and I realise that we should have had more rules for you. At all times we should have known where you were, and who you were with. We should never have allowed you to spend time alone with a boy. Anytime you went to town, Joy or Eunice should have been with you. We should have had those rules, no matter if people called us 'old-fashioned parents.' But now it's too late to discuss all that. I'm just saying: Part of the guilt is yours, and part is ours as parents."

"But Mom, I didn't think I could get pregnant."

Suddenly I realised how foolish that statement was.

Both of us were quiet for a moment. Then Mom looked up at me and cried as she said, "Why did you do it, Sindie? *Why?* I had so much trust in you, and so much hope for your future education."

"I'm sorry, Mom, . . . but I know 'sorry' doesn't change anything."

"Sindie," Mother's voice became softer, "the thought I've had again and again is: I love you. No matter what, I love you."

"Oh Mom, I love you too. Believe me, I didn't do this to hurt you. I don't know why I did it." We both burst into fresh tears and hugged each other tightly.

Drying her eyes, Mom became more practical. "I must take you to the doctor. Also, your Dad and I must speak with the boy's parents."

"He told me that he will deny that he's the father."

"Nevertheless, the adults in both families must discuss the whole matter."

I nodded.

Dinner that evening was so painful. We sat around the same table eating the same food, but nothing was the same. Dad was quiet as usual, but his quietness seemed *cold.* He could not make himself look at me.

I went to bed early, wanting to avoid contact with my family. Although they didn't separate themselves from me, I felt I must separate myself from them. I didn't deserve to be part of such a good family.

Surprisingly, just a few weeks ago I had told Ruth, "My family is unloving." Now I realise that isn't true. The love has always been there . . . I just didn't see it.

* * * * * * *

The sign said Pre-Natal Clinic. As Mom and I entered the crowded room, I opened my mouth to speak to the nurse, but Mom spoke first, giving her my name. The nurse gave Mom a form to fill in. Then I followed Mom as she chose seats for us. I felt foolish, like a little child who could do nothing for herself.

We sat down and Mom began filling in the form for me. "Mother, I can do that myself," I whispered. "I'm a big girl."

Mom looked hurt. "Of course you can do it, Sindie. I wasn't thinking." She handed me the form and pen.

But then I failed to answer the questions. The form asked for the address of my father's employment, etc. So I had to let Mom finish filling it in.

While she returned it to the nurse, I tried to look down at the floor, but my eyes were too interested in all the pregnant women in the room. Never before had I seen so many big stomachs! I wondered how the women looked before their bodies became so ugly.

Then I thought: *How will I look in a few more months?* The thought disgusted me! I won't be able to wear any of my fashion clothes.

When the nurse called my name, I was glad that Mom didn't come with me. I walked quietly across the room, hoping not to attract attention.

The elderly nurse led me to a small room where she weighed me. Then she gave me a plastic cup. "Fill this with urine," she said, pointing to a toilet.

How I hate handing someone a cup of my urine!

Next, the nurse told me I must undress. She handed me a white gown and led me to a small dressing room.

When I came out of the room wearing nothing but the gown, I felt nearly naked.

"Sit here," the nurse pointed to a tall, white stool.

She checked my blood pressure. "Why have you come?" she asked, like she didn't know.

"I'm pregnant," I answered in an innocent voice.

"When was your last menstrual period?"

"About the 28th of November."

She looked at the form Mom had filled in, probably to check my age. Then she looked back at me and raised her eyebrows as if to say, "Why'd you start so *young?"*

She turned and left the room. I was not sorry to see her go.

A minute later the doctor rushed into the room and said with a big smile, "Hello, Sindie. I'm Dr Walmon. How are you?"

"I'm fine, Doctor." I was glad he wasn't sour like that nurse.

"I understand you're expecting a baby." As he was speaking, he showed me where to lie down, and he began feeling my breasts with his cold hands. Then he said, "Now, Sindie, I'm going to examine your uterus."

Just then a nurse came in — not the sour one, but a young one wearing modern glasses.

"This is Sindie," the doctor told her.

"Hi, Sindie. I'm Mary," she said brightly.

"Glad to meet you," I smiled.

"Sindie," she said, "you must move down to the end of the table and get your feet up into these metal arms so the doctor can examine you."

When she had finished helping me into position, my naked buttocks were at the end of the table. My feet were held high by the two metal arms, and my legs were spread far apart. How could anyone be so *naked?*

The doctor picked up a thing that looked like a large metal duck-bill. "This is called a speculum," he said. "As I put it inside you, it will hold your vagina open so that I can take a small sample from your cervix for a pap-smear."

"Can you tell me what a 'pap-smear' is?" I hoped that if I continued talking, I'd be able to forget my nakedness.

"A pap-smear is a test for a disease called cancer of the cervix."

"But, Doctor, don't you think I'm too young to have that kind of cancer?" It sounded like a disease for a woman — not a girl.

"No, you're not too young. Some girls get this kind of cancer, especially those who start having sex at a young age — and very especially those who have several sex-partners."

"Oh," is all I said. I nearly told him that I didn't have 'several sex-partners.' But I decided not to mention the subject. Anyway, I couldn't deny that I began having sex at a very young age.

Then the doctor removed the speculum, put a glove on his hand, and put his hand inside my vagina.

It hurt!

He told me to relax. How could I? How could any girl relax with a man's hand inside her?

"Sindie, you are three months pregnant. Now the nurse is going to take a little of your blood so that we can see if you have any Sexually Transmitted Disease."

"Doctor, I couldn't have HIV or any other sex-disease because there was only one guy I ever slept with, and he didn't have any of those . . . ."

"You can't be sure that he didn't, Sindie. That's why we must test your blood. After the nurse takes your blood, you can dress. Then I'll come back and tell you what you must do."

As I finished dressing, he came hurrying back into the room and immediately started talking. "Sindie, I must tell you straight, your body is not yet ready to produce a baby. Why? Because you are so young. Actually, you are still a child yourself. You haven't yet finished growing. When a young girl (like you) is pregnant, there is the danger that she or the baby may not survive the birth process.

"So, Sindie, listen to me. Starting today be very careful to eat properly. Remember: the baby inside you is eating that same food. Sweets are not good for a baby. You want your baby to be healthy. So, eat three good meals every day. Eggs, beans, milk, raw vegetables and fruit are good. Avoid sugar and salt. Drink a lot of water. Now, do you have any questions?"

My mind was spinning. So many facts! "No, I guess not."

"Okay, Sindie. I'll see you next month."

"Thanks, Doctor."

12

My second visit to Dr Walmon wasn't so bad. I didn't need to take off any clothes. He told me to lift my dress and lie down. Then he put a stethoscope in his ears and listened to my stomach.

"I don't hear anything yet," he said with a smile. "Probably next time I'll hear the baby's heart-beat. By the middle of May you will begin to feel the baby move. Any question?"

"Yes, Doctor. May I sleep on my stomach?"

"It won't hurt the baby. But I suggest that you sleep on your side. Okay?"

I nodded.

"Right. I'll see you next month. Eat the right foods and drink plenty of water," he said over his shoulder as he rushed out.

As I was leaving I realised: I enjoy talking to the doctor. He understands me. In fact, he is the *only* one I feel free to talk to.

When I'm near Mom, I don't know if I should behave like her little daughter, or a grown woman.

I've been avoiding Ruth. I don't want to give her the chance to tell me that she never wants to see me again.

And Joy? She is the only one at school who knows that I'm pregnant. She's still my friend, but I'm sure she hates walking to school with me. We no longer have anything to talk about. We can't talk about the sports she's doing, because then I feel left out. And I don't like to talk about the baby because that brings up the subject of sex.

"Tell me," Joy said in a whisper as we were walking to school yesterday, "is it fun?"

"Is what fun?" I asked, confused.

"You know . . . when a girl lets a boy. . . ."

"No, it was not fun," I said impatiently.

"Then . . . why did you . . . ?"

"I don't know. I hoped it would be pleasant and wonderful . . . like ice cream."

She looked confused as she repeated, "*Ice cream?*"

"Oh, just forget it!" My voice was so harsh, neither of us said another word until we reached school.

* * * * * * *

In Mr Sanka's class the students never behave well. They pass notes to each other and whisper, but he never notices anything. His dry voice just talks on and on. I think he really believes we are listening to him.

All my friends are surprised that I no longer join in the fun. Instead, I just sit quietly, using my jersey to hide my growing stomach. And while Mr Sanka talks about flowers and frogs, my mind just thinks about the baby. Last week I began feeling him (or her) move. Ever since then, the baby is always on my mind. At night before I fall asleep, I feel a special closeness to him.

Often I wonder: Who will the baby look like? How will I take care of him? Will Mom quit her job and care for my baby? Or will Ben change his mind and take the baby... and me? When should I drop out of school? It will be nice to avoid dry teachers like Mr Sanka. But what will I do all day at home that will be less dry?

"Sindie!"

Suddenly I realised: Mr Sanka has been calling my name many times. Everyone is looking at me!

"*Sindie,* do you even know what question I asked you? Why don't you listen to me? Please tell the class what you are so busy thinking about."

It was my first time to see Mr Sanka angry. And at *me!*

Without waiting for an answer, he added, "You will stay here during break and study the chapter in your textbook on flowering plants."

I nodded in agreement and felt relief when everyone's eyes finally turned from me back to Mr Sanka.

By lunch-time Joy knew all about it. "I hear you got into trouble with Sanka," she said with laughter in her eyes.

I didn't feel like talking about it, so I just said, "It was *so* embarrassing!"

"Just forget it," she gave me a quick hug. Then she added, "Listen, I have an idea. After school today please come home with me. You haven't been to my house for a month. We can fry hamburgers... like we used to."

Poor Joy, still trying to be nice to me. But what else did I have to do? "Sure, Joy. I'd love to."

"Are hamburgers okay for you?" she put her hand on her stomach.

"Yes, hamburgers are fine," I said impatiently. I feel so tired of being *different* from other girls.

* * * * * * *

My mouth watered as Joy and I poured tomato sauce on our hamburgers. "I;m sure the baby is going to enjoy this hamburger," I said, patting the round bump under my dress.

Then I wished I had never mentioned 'baby,' because it started Joy asking questions — the very questions I was tired of thinking about.

"Who will take care of your baby?" she asked as she took her first bite.

"I can care for it myself. I love babies. They are sweet, and nice to hold. And my baby will love me. I need that."

"Sindie, do you really think life will be wonderful with a baby? I mean at your age . . . ."

"No, I don't think it will be wonderful. Life always has ups and downs. But I'm sure a baby will make my life more interesting."

Joy shook her head. "Sindie, babies don't make a girl's life interesting. With a baby to care for, how much fun can you have with the other girls? You'll be lonely. And if you take care of the baby yourself, you'll never finish school or go to university. No, Sindie, you must think of someone else to care for your baby."

"Who? I doubt if Mom will leave her job. The best idea I can think of is: I'll get a job and hire a woman to watch my baby while I work."

"But you have no training." Joy said as she took another bite. "So, what job will you get? And do you really want a hired woman to care for your child?"

"Oh stop preaching! I see your problem — you hate children!"

"I do not! But now I enjoy having friends my own age. After I marry, then I will want a baby."

"Now I see why you're angry. You're jealous because I'm going to have a baby before you."

"Hah! I'm not jealous. Listen to me. I said that I want a baby after I *marry.* That means, when I have a *husband.*"

"Who says I'll never have a husband?"

"Do you think guys will be very interested in a girl who has another guy's baby?"

My eyes spit fire. "What makes *you* such an expert?"

Joy looked down at the floor. Her voice turned gentle. "My brother is interested in Priscilla. He keeps telling me, 'I want to marry her . . . but I wish she didn't have that other guy's child.'"

"But Joy," I said softly, "why do you doubt that Ben will marry me? It's *his* child."

Joy was silent. Her face looked like she felt sorry for me.

"You know," I continued, "in my heart I'm sure that Ben will come back and marry me. We will have a nice wedding, move into a cosy flat, and have a fun life together."

"Sindie, don't you see that those are just *dreams?* You must wake up!"

"Why can't it be that way?" I begged.

"Listen, Sindie. Ben never really loved you."

The words cut like a knife into my pain-filled heart. *"What do you mean by that?"* I asked hotly.

"Oh, Sindie, I never wanted to tell you."

"Tell me what?" I feared what she would say.

"During the holiday, while you were looking only at Ben, his eyes were busy looking at other girls."

"What *proof* do you have?" My tears began to flow.

"Sindie, from the beginning of holiday until the end, Ben often phoned *me,* trying to sweet-talk me!"

Joy cried with me.

"Why didn't you *tell* me?" I sobbed.

"I didn't realise that you two were sleeping together. I mean . . . I never thought you'd get pregnant. I told myself, 'Ben will leave at the end of holiday, and then Sindie can just forget him.' "

I threw my arms around her for support as we cried together. Oh, how I hated Ben! But oh, how I wanted him to come back and love me the way he used to . . . or like I *thought* he used to! He has spoiled my life. Why did I allow him to *use* me? How could I have been so *blind?*

"Oh, Joy. . ." I cried. "You're right. All my hopes about Ben are just *dreams.* And now I don't want to wake up. I've been such a fool!"

* * * * * * *

Pain fills my heart. I'm surprised it can still beat under the terrible weight. I no longer cry very often, but when I do cry, my tears are angry and hateful.

I don't care if I ever eat again. Food is tasteless.

I've burned every picture of Ben.

How could he use me and then drop me like a piece of rubbish? He told me, "It's like ice cream." Now I feel like a used ice cream dish . . . dirty and empty.

He promised to love me forever. I gave him my body. He's father to our baby. I want him to love me. I *need* him to love me.

Each day the terrible hole in my heart grows larger.

I've quit school. All the staff and students know that I'm pregnant. I can no longer hide it.

Most of the time I stay in the house. I hate to walk in town because people pass remarks about how young I am to have such a stomach.

I was glad one day when five girls from school came to visit me here at home. They seemed really excited about my pregnancy. All of them wanted to touch my stomach.

But not one of them wants to be my friend.

On my birthday I received four presents from various relatives. Each present was a pair of *socks!* Obviously, no one knows what to buy a pregnant girl who shouldn't be pregnant.

* * * * * * *

Yesterday I told myself: *I must phone Ben. I can't live another day without his loving support.*

The telephone receiver shook in my hand.

"Hello," a girl's voice answered. It was Ben's sister.

"Hello. May I speak to Ben?"

She paused a moment, probably trying to guess who I was. "He went to a party with a pretty girl — I can't remember her name. Do you wish to leave a message?"

"No. Good-bye."

I anger I ran to my room and I threw my pillow against the wall as hard as I could.

I refused to eat dinner . . . I had tears instead.

13

Today I decided to visit Ruth. For the past two months she's been phoning each week, but I've never talked to her. I always let Eunice answer the phone. I've trained her to tell everyone, "Sindie isn't home."

I now feel so miserable, even if Ruth scolds and rejects me, it won't matter. I'm used to that. Everyone has rejected me.

Looking in my mirror, I saw an angry face topped by uncombed hair. I got my hair into shape, and five minutes later I was walking through cold rain to Ruth's house. By the time I arrived, my feet and stomach were soaked. Dad's old raincoat protected the rest of me.

Ruth's eyes danced with joy when she saw me. "*Sindie! Come in! Come right in!*" She threw her arms around me, hugging me tightly. And I was still wearing the wet coat!

She hung up my coat as I chose a hard chair. (Soft chairs are too difficult for me to get up out of.) Little Joel came running to me. His hugs helped to fill the huge hole in my heart.

Ruth removed Joel's toys from the chair in front of me and sat down. We talked lightly for a while, and then she asked, "How's your family?"

"I guess they're okay," I shrugged my shoulders.

"How are they accepting your present situation?"

"I could tell you lies," my voice turned bitter. "I could tell you, 'Eunice is a sweet sister who refuses to join her friends when they joke about me.' I could tell you, 'My brother has taken his mind off soccer for a minute so that he could say something kind to me.' And I could tell you, 'Dad has forgiven me.'"

Ruth remained silent, her face concerned.

"I could tell you all those things," I continued, "but it would be a big lie."

"What's the truth?" Ruth gently asked as she picked up Joel and held him in her lap.

Taking a deep breath I began, "When Eunice is with her friends, she acts like she doesn't know me.

"My brother never puts down his soccer magazine long enough to speak to me about anything.

"And Dad . . . usually he just looks at me without saying a word. Probably if he did say something, it would be hurtful."

I paused a moment, trying to think of what Dad might say. "I guess it's better that he's just quiet."

"What do you *want* them to do?" Ruth asked, as Joel was falling asleep in her arms.

"I want them to *accept* me. That's all I want." I wiped a tear from one eye. "I want them to forgive me and love me as a member of the family."

Ruth nodded. I knew she understood. When she spoke, her voice was soft and warm. "I'm sorry you feel that no one accepts you. But there is a Father in heaven who would be happy to accept you. He is just waiting for you to choose to be his child."

"Choose? Why must I choose? I've always been His child . . . haven't I? Aren't we all God's children?"

Ruth smiled. "God created us all. He wants us to be His children. But people turn their backs on Him."

Joel was now asleep, and so Ruth whispered, "Excuse me," and gently carried him to his bed.

While she was away, I suddenly realised: I have turned my back on God! Every day of my life I say and do sinful things.

When Ruth returned, she was carrying a tray with a tea pot and two cups. As she poured mine, I asked, "So, how can a person become a child of God?"

"You ask Him to forgive your sins, and you accept Him as Master of your life."

"What's the advantage of doing that?" I asked doubtfully.

"There are many advantages. When we accept God, He gives us peace in life's troubles. He promises us eternal life. There are so many things that a perfect Father can give to His children."

"That's the problem," I said hopelessly. "He's 'perfect.' He wouldn't want *me* to be His child."

"What do you mean?" Ruth asked.

"Just look at me!" I pointed to my stomach. "I could never be the child of a *perfect* Father. And this big stomach is not my only sin. The way I talk and behave; I'm sure I do many sins every day. I'm not nearly good enough to be His child."

Ruth's face softened. "Sindie, no one is good enough.

All of us humans should suffer in hell for our sins, but God has made a way for us to receive heaven. He sent His Son, Jesus, to suffer in our place. Now anyone will be washed clean if he/she chooses to trust in Jesus."

Time flew as we talked. For the first time in my life, I listened with interest.

In the past I'd heard preachers shout, *"Jesus died for us!"* I always told myself, "Those are just religious words."

But now as Ruth talked, I began to see it. Yes, I should be separated from God forever in hell . . . but I can become God's child and live with Him forever. Why? Because Jesus suffered for the sins I've done. He died for *me!*

"Ruth," my voice was shaking. "I want to take Jesus and be a child of God . . . like you."

"I'm glad, Sindie. Just tell Him that right now."

"Tell Him? You mean . . . pray? I don't know how. I can't pray."

"Yes, you can. Just talk to God."

"But how?"

"Simply say to Him whatever you want to say."

I looked down at the floor and shut my eyes tightly. "God I admit that I'm sinful. I don't know how to say this, but I need Jesus. I believe He died for me. Please wash me clean. Thank you for heaven. And please begin changing me into the kind of person you want me to be. Amen."

Everyone has sinned.
(Romans 3:23)

Your sins should send you to hell.
(Romans 6:23)

But,
God so loved the world that he gave his only Son, so that anyone who believes in him will not perish, but will have eternal life.
(John 3:16
John 1:12,
1 Peter 3:18,
Romans 5:6-8,
Isaiah 53:5-6,
1 John 5:13)

I feared that I had said all the wrong things. And it didn't even sound like a prayer should sound.

Ruth sat close to me, held my hand and said very simply, "Dear Lord, you've heard all my prayers for Sindie, and today you've answered them. Thank you so much. We love you. Amen."

I opened my eyes. "It's gone!" I exclaimed.

"What's gone?" Ruth questioned.

"The terrible hole in my heart . . . it's finally gone!" I looked at her with a bright smile on my face.

She gave me a long, tight hug.

The phone rang, interrupting our quiet joy. "It's your sister," Ruth said.

"Hello, Eunice, what's new?" I said cheerfully.

Her voice was serious. "He asked me to tell you . . . I mean Ben . . . he's here in town. He phoned from Dan's. He wants to see you there."

14

The rain had stopped. As I walked, I kept thinking about Ben. Why did he come? What will he say?

I shook with both fear and excitement. Maybe he will take me to his home where we will have a beautiful wedding.

As I hurried along the pavement, I was sure everyone who walked past me could hear my heart pounding.

I decided to approach Dan's from the back so that I could see Ben before he saw me.

When I saw him, I stood still. My memory raced back. I remembered the day — months ago — when I first saw him standing right there. Now he looked even more handsome. His blue, silk shirt made him look especially warm and hugable.

His head was turned the other direction, yet I knew his eyes were full of self-confidence as always. He looked so handsome . . . so respectable. I wanted to throw my arms around him. At the same time, I wanted to throw a big stone at him.

Instead, I walked slowly to him and said, "Good afternoon, Ben."

He turned and saw me. Immediately his eyes grew wide as he looked at my face . . . then my stomach.

His self-confidence totally disappeared. I didn't know that Ben could be nervous, yet now his tongue started vibrating wildly. "I never . . . uh . . . never . . . ."

His eyes continued to stare about half a metre below my chin. His voice was so unlike the smooth voice I was used to.

Again he tried to speak, his arm swinging awkwardly, "I didn't expect you to look like . . . uh . . . this."

I wanted to ask: How did you expect a pregnant girl to look? Instead, I forced myself to be polite. "How are you?" I asked.

Again he tried to look me in the eye, but there seemed to be a magnet pulling his eyes down to stare at my very round stomach. "I'm fine . . . I guess."

He looked all around to be sure no one was watching us. Then, as he began talking, I could see that he had memorized every word. He sounded like a school-child reciting a poem.

"Sindie, I came for two reasons. I've brought you a birthday present, and the other thing is . . . I've decided; I can never tell anyone that I'm the father of your baby. I'm not ready for the responsibility of a child."

Anger hit me like a wave of the sea. I threw words at him like stones. "That's *wonderful!* Our child will grow up without his father . . . why? . . . because you want to enjoy a no-responsibility life!"

I blinked my eyes quickly. I didn't want to lose my battle with tears.

Confused, he turned to walk away. Then he stopped and turned back to face me again. His shaking hand held a pretty little box. "I nearly forgot to give you this," he said nervously.

My mouth said, "Thanks," but my heart screamed: *"Does this pay for what he's doing to me and to our child?"*

Then . . . he left.

As I watched him walk away with his head down, I knew I would never see him again.

Suddenly I just wanted to be home. I turned and walked there as fast as my big body would allow.

No one was home, so I just sat on my bed and let my tears drip onto the pretty little box. Red roses decorated the wrapping paper. I wiped my eyes. Then I slowly pulled off the ribbon and opening the box.

Angrily I threw the *socks* as far as I could. Then I shouted through fresh tears, "Ben, how can you leave me like this?!"

* * * * * * *

I thought I'd never want another gift from anyone, but now Ruth has given me two that I really like. The first and best is a Bible. The second is a notebook.

In my whole life I've never read any part of the Bible, until now. This week I've read it every morning. Ruth suggested that I begin with the book of John. After reading some verses, I write comments in my notebook. Ruth reads the same verses, and later in the day we discuss what we've read.

It's exciting! I'm amazed to find that the Bible is interesting!

I'm learning so much about the way Jesus wants me to live. Now, when I feel like scolding Eunice, my mind recalls the words, "Love others as I love you."

By the way, Eunice has changed. She's more kind to me. Often she puts her hand on my stomach, waiting for the baby to kick. She enjoys that. I think loving the baby is her way of loving me.

Even my brother is becoming friendly. Sometimes he actually says, "Good morning," and a few times even, "How are you?" For him, that's progress!

Ruth tells me, "Sindie, ***you*** are the one who is changing, and that makes it easier for your family to show love to you."

Yesterday Dad came home from work and walked over to where I was sewing. As he sat beside me, I felt fearful and kept my eyes down on my work.

"Sindie," his voice was unusually soft, "I understand how heartbroken you feel. But I want you to know: We don't look down on you. We love you."

He put his big hand on my shoulder for a moment; then he stood and walked away.

I smiled. That was Dad's way of saying that he forgives me.

However, my life has two big problems. The first is Joy. Last week I told her how Ruth helped me to become a Christian. I tried to say, "Jesus forgave me and . . . ."

Before I could finish, Joy just laughed. But then she said, "Sindie, you certainly have *changed.* You are more cheerful. Now I enjoy spending time with you. It seems you have something good to look forward to — a hope, or something."

Then she said sadly, "You seem to have a secret that you can't share with me."

"That's not true, Joy. I can share everything. You too can receive eternal life by believing in . . . ."

Joy stopped me by shaking her head. "No, Sindie. My life is okay. I don't need religion."

I feel disappointed that Joy is not quick to accept

Christ. I must keep on praying for her, like Ruth did for me.

My second problem is Mother. She forces me to discuss things I'm trying not to think about.

This morning my back hurt terribly as I sat at the sewing machine making a baby-blanket. Suddenly Mom entered the room and said. "Sindie, we really must discuss what we will do if Ben's family refuses to take the baby."

Impatiently I let the scissors drop on the table. "Please, Mom, I don't feel like talking about it now." I pulled out pins, getting ready to sew again.

As if she hadn't heard me, she forced a smile and continued. "When your dad and I phoned Ben's parents, they said, *'We can't believe that our son is the father of any baby.'* We must talk to them again, but it seems they don't want the baby. Therefore I hope the baby will stay with us instead of them, because a child needs to feel loved. Don't you agree?"

I hoped that if I didn't answer, maybe she would stop talking. My back-pain was growing worse. It wasn't the time to discuss all this.

However, she just carried on, saying the same things I'd heard her say dozens of times. "If the child stays with us, I have no idea who will take care of it. I can't quit my job. Perhaps we could hire someone, but that's expensive now-a-days. And a child really should be cared for by its mother. But if you care for the child, how will you finish school? And university will be out of the question. Oh Sindie, you know how your dad and I have hoped that you would graduate, but now. . . ."

"Mother, please," I finally exclaimed. "Can't we discuss this another day? My back hurts . . . ."

"Of course, Dear," she forced another smile. "Just

remember, I'm always available to talk . . . any time."

"Yes, Mom." My smile was weak.

After she left I realised: I must do better at loving my mother. I hope my whole family will believe in Jesus, but how will that happen unless they see a change in me?

* * * * * * *

"How's everything?" Dr Walmon asked cheerfully while listening to my stomach.

I told him about my back pains. He said, "Don't worry, that's normal during pregnancy." He called everything I mentioned "normal". . . my leaking breasts, and even the ugly lines on my stomach.

Then I felt I must tell him, "Honestly, Doctor, I'm *very* tired of this big stomach."

He smiled understandingly. "That's normal, too. But you won't need to wait much longer. I suspect you'll deliver about the 10th of September."

"*Suspect?* You mean, you don't know for sure?"

He laughed. "No one can know that. Next time you come here I'll do another vaginal exam. That will help me to predict your delivery date more accurately."

I said a half-hearted, "Okay, Doctor."

"See you in two weeks," he smiled.

15

Nearly the whole night I couldn't sleep because of constant pain in my back.

05:30 hours. As the sun appeared, my abdomen began to squeeze, and the pain in my back increased. Walking around the room helped a little.

I still felt like this must be happening to someone else — not me. My brain tried to think: Is this real? Am I really going to give birth? How will I feel when I hold my very own baby?

Then pain hit me so hard that I had to bend over.

I felt very afraid as I realised: I have no idea what it's like to give birth. I'm entering a world I've never known before — a world of fear and pain — and perhaps joy.

05:45 hours. By now I realised I was having "contractions." Each time a contraction hit me, the pain forced me to stop walking and bend over.

I knew Mom would wake up soon. I hated to disturb her busy life. Why didn't the baby come on a weekend so that she wouldn't need to miss work?

10:00 hours. In the hospital I felt less afraid. The nurse showed me how to breathe deeply during a contraction. That reduced the pain.

Mom sat patiently beside me. I knew by the look in her eyes that she felt each contraction with me.

Dr Walmon came, looked inside my vagina, and said, "Your cervix is open only 3 cm. It must be open 10 cm before the baby can come out. So the birth will probably be in the afternoon."

I could not imagine how *long* this day would be!

11:00 hours. An overweight nurse entered carrying a tray of medical things. "Your name Sindie?" her voice was harsh and uncaring. "I've come to *prep* you."

I quickly looked at Mom, then back to the nurse. "I don't know what…"

"I'm going to shave you and give you an enema," she interrupted.

My face twisted into a frown. Why must giving birth be so disgusting?

The nurse noticed my displeasure and added, "It's not that bad. The enema will clean your intestine. You don't want a smelly mess when you push the baby out."

Then a wave of pain hit me. I grabbed the bed tightly with both hands.

When the pain was gone, the nurse shaved me while saying, "A few weeks after delivery, you may still be bleeding. Then you'll be glad not to have this pubic hair."

She pushed the enema tube up my rectum. Water from the bottle rushed inside me.

"I can't hold it, I can't hold it," I pleaded.

"You can and you will!" she said sternly. "Sit on that toilet and hold the water in as long as possible. Then let everything come out."

13:00 hours. I heard them bringing food, and I told myself, "After a miserable morning, at least I'll get a nice lunch." But the nurse said, "Sindie, you get nothing. If you eat, you will vomit when your contractions get harder."

Harder? I didn't want to believe they could get any harder!

14:00 hours. A nurse looked in my vagina and said, "Your cervix is now 5 cm." Only half-way!

For the first time in my life, I could not control my body. During each contraction, my abdomen muscles pulled tightly—without my permission. The pain always grew and grew... then my muscles would relax and I could rest for some moments . . . until the next one came.

Every contraction was harder than the previous one. I kept trying not to scream or cry. Finally I begged the nurse, "Please give me medicine for pain."

"No, you'll be okay," she said without feeling.

I looked into my mother's eyes, silently begging for help. Her eyes were filled with love . . . and remembering.

During the next contraction I felt something wet and warm. "Is that blood?" I cried in fear.

The nurse took a quick look. "No. Your water broke."

"My what?"

"The water bag around your baby—it broke. Now your contractions will come harder and faster."

15:00 hours. I was now open 7 cm. I no longer cared. I was in such pain.

The way Mother stared at me made me afraid. Sometimes I wished she would go and leave me alone.

Dr Walmon came in for a very quick check. Then he rushed out again.

I was tired of all this. I wanted to go home and forget it.

Mother left to get a cup of tea. When she was gone, suddenly I hoped she would hurry back.

16:00 hours. I told the nurse, "I need to go to the toilet. *Right now!*"

"No you don't," she said. "That feeling is the baby moving down your vagina. During your next contraction, push hard. I'm going to call the midwife."

16:05 hours. Soon the midwife entered the room, quickly examined me, and said with authority, "It's time. I can see the baby's head at the entrance to your vagina. Let's take you to the Delivery Room."

She pushed my bed down the passage. I had so few clothes on, normally I would have felt embarrassed. But now I didn't care.

In the Delivery Room they moved me to a white table. Then the midwife held a stethoscope on my stomach, listening for the baby's heartbeat. She tried again and again. Finally she whispered to the nurse, "Call the doctor. Hurry!"

Dr Walmon rushed in and began listening to my stomach. I could see worry growing on his face.

I was full of fear. I remembered hearing that very young mothers often deliver dead babies; and sometimes the mother dies too.

Then I felt much stretching and movement as the baby's head came out.

"Push again," Dr Walmon encouraged.

I pushed with all my remaining strength. The baby came sliding out. I cried with relief.

Then I heard another crying — a baby — *my* baby! Thank God!

"What a beautiful boy!" nurses were exclaiming.

A nurse pushed on my flat stomach and pulled on the umbilical cord. "The placenta will come out now," she told me.

I had forgotten about the placenta. As it came out, it looked ugly red and black.

Then they moved me to my bed, put my baby in my arms, and pushed the bed to my room. I lay there thanking God for the precious new life sleeping on my breast.

I wanted to sleep too, but my mind refused to be quiet. Now that my lovely baby was born, I wanted my heart to be full of pure joy. But my joy was mixed with a dark, lonely feeling.

Will Ben feel any joy to know that he has a son? Years from now, will he be giving our son the love and encouragement that every boy needs from his father?

Lord, please help me in my battle to forgive Ben.

I'm so thankful that I refused abortion. And that I turned to God.

What a different person I am now! A year ago I was searching for love. I felt I was receiving too little love from my parents, and I didn't believe in God's love. Because I was so hungry for love, I wanted to believe that Ben loved me. And I was foolish enough to think that I could find love by breaking God's law for sex.

Now, I'm no longer searching for love. Perhaps I will receive very little love from my friends and relatives; but God loves me!

Oh why didn't I listen to Ruth years ago when she tried to tell me about God? Instead, I chose to go my own way. And now, even as I hold my precious baby, my heart is heavy.

Because I ignored God, I've changed from a girl to a woman much too soon. I wish I could go back and be a girl again. I don't want to be a woman — not yet.

What will my future be? Will I ever have a husband and children? One thing I know is: I will encourage my children (and all children) to accept Christ while they are young — before they get into trouble. I'll tell teenage young people to enjoy doing Christian work together — in a group. I'll warn girls not to spend time alone with a boy.

Why did I learn that too late?

I cannot change my past. Now I'm just glad to be God's child. I want to serve Him by telling people everywhere how to receive eternal life. And I want to be a wonderful mother to my son.

After Sindie dies, she will stand before God. On that day, Satan will point at her and say, "Sindie, you sinned. Come to hell forever."

But Jesus will say, "At age 16 Sindie asked me to be her Saviour and Lord. On the cross I suffered for her sins. Come, Sindie, enjoy heaven with me forever (John 3:36). And thank you, Sindie, for spending your life encouraging children and adults to receive me as Saviour. Here is your eternal reward." (Matt. 28:19-20, 1 Corinth. 2:9, Rev. 22:12)

To everyone who reads this book we say: Accept Christ and serve him. One good way to serve him is: Teach the Bible to children and young people. When they reach age 12, they should be able to say, "I have taken Jesus as my Saviour. I understand his law for sex. I will obey him."

Then they will avoid the sorrows Sindie faced.

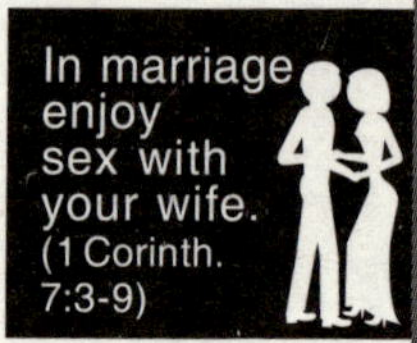

Note to men: Be an excellent father to your children. Don't copy Ben. The Bible says: God punishes fathers who don't take good care of their children. (Study 1 Samuel 2:22 and 3:12-13.)

Have children within marriage—not outside. Stay with your wife and kids. Help your kids and other kids to receive Jesus and learn the Bible. (Study Deut. 6:6-7, 1 Tim. 5:8, Luke 18:16)

A Letter from a Reader

Dear Bruce and Carol,

Your book, 'Kiss me Sweet Baby,' *touched my heart. As I read it, I began to realise that God loves me. I decided to become a real Christian, like Sindie. Page 80 really helped me!*

I'm still young (age 13). I'm glad I read this book before getting into trouble. I see many girls who are in deep trouble because of sins they do with boys. Their boyfriends are exactly like Ben.

Since the day I accepted Christ, I'm more careful to respect my mother, and I attend church with her. She's very, very happy about that!

I'm busy telling my friends how they can become Christians. They all want to read 'Kiss me Sweet Baby.' *So I let them borrow my copy.*

My mother bought her own copy. She tells every mother to read it.

Thanks for writing this book that has opened my eyes and started me on the Christian road.

In Christ's love,
Rachel

Other titles available by Bruce Britten:

For all serious Christians. Power to do God's work!

A book for married people, not for single young people.

Young people find in this book the keys to true love.

Power for you to be a man of God...a woman of God.

AFRICA
STUDY
BIBLE
NLT

OASIS INTERNATIONAL

is the proud publisher
of many great titles to help inform your Christian life!
Visit oasisint.net to learn more.

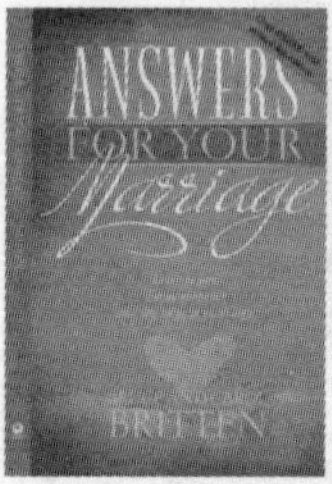

Answers for your Marriage
Bruce & Carol Britten

African Traditional Religion
in Biblical Perspective
Richard Gehman

A Pre-Marriage Counselling
Handbook
Alan & Donna Goerz

African Traditional Religion
and Christian Counseling
Karl Grebe & Wilfred Fon

Learning to Lead
Richard Gehman

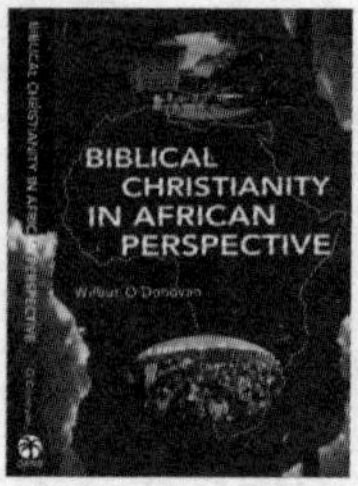

Biblical Christianity in
African Perspective
Wilber O'Donovan

Conflict Resolution
in the Church
Philip Morrison & Chris Mwala'a

Love & Marriage
Bruce & Carol Britten

Biblical Christianity in
Modern Africa
Wilber O'Donovan

Sharing the Gospel with
Muslims
John Gilchrist

OASIS INTERNATIONAL LIMITED
Satisfying Africa's Thirst for God's Word

oasisint.net
facebook.com/OasisIntLtd
info@oasisint.net